Be My Daddy

A Story of Compassion and Rescue

Stanley Barnes
with Victor Maxwell

Be My Daddy

ISBN 978-1-909751-16-3

*Proceeds from the sale of this book will be
donated to The Deborah House Project*

Cover photo © Eric Stitt

Printed by: J C Print Limited
Email: info@jcprint.net

Contents

Page

Preface

It gives me great pleasure to be identified with this book detailing the amazing stories of lives that have been touched and transformed by the grace of God.

I have known the Rev. Stanley and Mrs. Ina Barnes for more than forty years and had the joy of working with them in Hillsborough Free Presbyterian Church.

I will always remember the impact the Rev. Barnes made on our church when he returned from Romania in February 1990. He spoke with a great passion of Pastor Eugen Groza and the underground church in Timisoara. After that I travelled with the Rev. Barnes and other friends from Hillsborough to help in the construction of the new Bethany Baptist Church. While there we were all deeply touched by the sad plight of orphaned, abandoned and abused children who were housed in drab institutions where they were bereft of any comfort, love or hope.

We all felt something had to be done for these deprived and neglected young people. The Rev. Barnes gave leadership to all of us at the Hillsborough Free Presbyterian Church in helping Pastor Eugen and his friends to acquire and develop the Deborah House Centre.

This expanding ministry of compassion is still giving new hope to many young ones who have been rescued from ruined backgrounds.

I am grateful that my family and I had a small part to play in the development of this work.

David Williamson, MBE

Chapter 1

Ready for Revolution

The dimly lit room might have reflected the sombre mood of the people, but it could not have concealed Pastor Eugen Groza's delight. He had a huge smile on his face as he stood behind a simple lectern strategically placed at the corner of an L-shaped room. This gave him the best vantage point from which to address his congregation. This modified house was the home of Bethany Baptist Church, Timisoara, Romania, and this was their Wednesday night prayer meeting in February 1990.

The elated young pastor spoke enthusiastically as he welcomed Rev. Stanley Barnes, the first foreign pastor to visit this house-church since the recent Romanian Revolution, which had had its beginning two months earlier a few miles away in the centre of their city, the pastor's elation was not only due to Stanley's visit to this fledging church. Eugen, his wife, Mihaela, and his congregation were still overjoyed that the long years of draconian oppression and persecution from the state were over. No longer did they need to fear Ceausescu's Securitate (Ceausescu's secret police), the infiltration of informers or the constant intimidation to which they had become accustomed for many years.

Stanley, the minister of Hillsborough Free Presbyterian Church, was part of a ministerial delegation which had arrived from

Northern Ireland for two purposes. Firstly, it was a fact-finding mission on the part of two British politicians who were travelling with the delegation. Secondly, it was to encourage and show solidarity with these persecuted, but recently liberated, Christian brethren. Although Stanley felt it was a privilege to be present at the church, he also found it to be a very humbling experience. He had never really known persecution firsthand in his long years of Christian ministry. Furthermore, until recently, he had been largely unaware of the plight of these Romanian believers. Now he stood before this group of assembled Christians who had not only suffered for years, but they also had recently risked their lives to gain the freedoms they were now enjoying.

Pastor Eugen Groza and the people of Timisoara would never forget Christmas 1989. The events that led up to that festive season still caused them to marvel at how quickly they had been liberated from more than forty years under the terrible scourge of communism that had inflicted poverty on the people and suppressed religious worship. The overthrow of atheistic communism had been an amazing answer to their prayers and those of Christians all over Romania.

Since the emergence of the Soviet Union's Mikhail Gorbachev and the introduction of his policy of Perestroika in 1987, many Romanians had been whispering about the winds of change that were sweeping across other eastern-bloc Communist countries. Through tiny peepholes into the outside world and by listening to outlawed radio stations, people learned that communist rule had already been toppled from East Germany to Bulgaria. They had also heard that in China, tanks had crushed mass democracy protests and public demonstrations.

The tyrannical leaders of the Romanian communist regime were also aware of these ongoing developments in Eastern Europe and were fearful of similar manifestations happening in their own country. No one doubted that the ruthless Nicolae Ceausescu would try to apply a "Chinese solution" to any uprising if the people dared to revolt against him. Therefore, through the army and Securitate he tightened his grip on maintaining his authority and power in an attempt to stifle any unrest. He ordered that special attention be focused on Christian leaders who had long been a source of defiance and resistance against the atheistic state.

After Nicolae Ceausescu had been elevated to power in 1965, he embarked on an insane campaign to leave his own retrograde mark on Romania. In the exercise of his authoritarian command he had destroyed the rich heritage of Bucharest's magnificent and classical architecture as he bulldozed his way through the heart of the nation's capital to construct his own avenues of concrete apartment blocks and government edifices. For over a century before World War II Bucharest had been looked upon as "the Paris of the East". Ceausescu's construction crews demolished all that was beautiful about the city. He not only robbed it of its pride and elegance, but he also drained the country of its wealth and resources to feed his insatiable appetite for his own egotistic grandeur.

In the heart of the city he embarked on one of the most controversial projects of his twenty-five-year rule: the construction of a gargantuan Stalinist-like edifice, which was to be named "The Palace of the Parliament". Described by some as a giant Stalinist wedding cake, at 350,000 square meters (3.77 million square feet), the palace is the second-largest administrative building in the world, conceding first place to only the Pentagon in Washington DC.

Besides imposing his ruthless stamp on the nation's standing in the world and draining its considerable assets, Nicolae Ceausescu and his communist leaders engineered ways of suppressing the Romanian population. Its borders were sealed, and movement of its people was greatly restricted. Westerners were generally denied access to Romania, and it was illegal for most Romanians to travel to the West or to make contact with Western people. News of the outside world was carefully controlled, filtered and prejudicially spun by the regime to give their own interpretation on international events.

Life under Ceausescu's rule for the average Romanian was tough. Shop shelves were frequently bare, and long queues outside these shops for daily necessities became a typical way of life. Food was rationed as were amenities such as water, electricity and gas. Ironically, there was almost full employment in Romania during those years, but virtually everyone was paid the same low wage with little or no distinction made for those who would normally be considered to be in professional positions. Most families in the cities were housed in drab grey apartment blocks which belonged to the state.

While the general populace was denied any semblance of a reasonable standard of living, the inner circle of Ceausescu's favoured elite enjoyed many luxuries of which most Romanians could only dream.

Added to all this, the regime did an astounding job of creating a society bereft of trust. It was reckoned that one Romanian citizen in every four was an informer for the government's secret police. Through this network of informers in all areas of society, academic, commercial and religious, the Securitate constantly monitored the general population. It was their strategy of suffocating any threat of an uprising against the ruling party.

Christian ministers became a prime target for the Securitate. They were routinely watched, followed, and checked, and an account was registered of their movements, contacts and influences. Pastors were required to give a weekly report about any visitors who might have attended their church. Many men of God ignored this government edict but paid the price for it. Church members and even some ministers were recruited by the Securitate to inform on their leaders. Consequently, many servants of God were repeatedly arrested, interrogated, harassed, imprisoned and even tortured. In his book, Tortured For Christ, Pastor Richard Wurmbrand gives a horrendous account of his years of suffering imprisonment, solitary confinement and physical torture because of his Christian faith.

In spite of the tyrannical and extreme measures the regime imposed on Christian churches and their leaders, they could not stop God's work or immobilise many dedicated servants of God. Under threat of imprisonment or even death these faithful men and women continued to serve their Lord in establishing house churches, running underground printing presses and zealously evangelising their communities. Ceausescu's government outlawed most of this activity, but God continued to bless His servants, and His work expanded and flourished despite the opposition.

For ten years Pastor Eugen Groza and his congregation at Bethany Baptist Church had experienced both aspects of these contrasting currents: government opposition and heavenly blessings. Founded as a house church in 1979, Bethany Baptist developed and was consolidated through the following decade by the faithful prayers of its members. They were repeatedly exposed to the same threats and opposition that were all too common throughout Romania. Pastor Eugen, who had been a student with Tom Lewis's Bible Education by Extension programme for ten years, was frequently arrested, interrogated and threatened. Their church gatherings were often disrupted, and every week they had to pay a fine because their meeting was deemed to be illegal.

Notwithstanding the disapproval of government authorities and hostility from the Securitate who hounded them, they continued to be steadfast in prayer and appealed to God for liberation from this totalitarian oppression.

Everything changed on Christmas Day 1989. Throughout the country unrest had been mounting for several days. In response to the arrest and maltreatment of Pastor Laszlo Tökes of the Romanian Reformed Church in the provincial city of Timisoara, hundreds of people converged on the city's central square to show their revulsion and disagreement. Pastor Tökes had dared to denounce the autocratic authorities. His lone and courageous voice became a thorn in the regime's side. On 15th December 1989, he was to be exiled to a remote village for having given an interview to a foreign television crew that had been smuggled into the country. Hundreds of loyal parishioners encircled his church on that date in an attempt to stop the pastor's arrest. Even though water cannons were turned on the protestors, hundreds more people and then thousands more, came into the streets to join in the protest.

The Revolution had begun.

Very soon masses of demonstrators filled the streets of Timisoara. This was most unusual for Romania, for the like of it had never happened before in Timisoara or any other town. Pastor Eugen accompanied members of his church and many other Christians to support the thousands who had gathered at the centre of the city. By this time this was a lot more than a protest against the arrest of a local pastor. This was a populist uprising that would soon explode into a nationwide revolt. For three days and three nights Eugen and his friends did not sleep. They sensed they were on the verge of a revolution.

That is exactly what happened. In Timisoara today, twelve monuments mark spots where dozens died. Many reprisals took place and bullet-pierced bodies were found in various places. The Securitate killed many more before fleeing to Bucharest. When Ceausescu addressed a 500,000 strong crowd from a balcony in Bucharest to denounce the Timisoara uprising, instead of acquiescing to his strong words as they had formerly done for years, the people, en-masse, revolted against him with chants of "Timisoara, Timisoara, Timisoara!"

The dictator beckoned with his hand and commanded the protesting multitude to be silent. "Be quiet! Be quiet!" he bellowed. When they refused to be silenced he commanded the army to open fire. Dozens of innocent Romanians died in the fracas that followed. Even with this the people refused to be muzzled or to comply with Ceausescu's dictates.

Subsequently, Ceausescu's dictatorship was overthrown. The Defence Ministry was secured by military commanders, most of whom had switched allegiance to side with the people. There was no way Romania was going back to the past.

Ceausescu fled north, stopping at a lakeside villa so his wife could grab her jewellery. His pilot either pretended mechanical problems or said that anti-aircraft radar was tracking them. They landed near Targoviste where they had a bodyguard hijack two cars. The couple sought refuge at a government nursery, but it was there that the army arrested them.

On Christmas Day 1989, an arrogant President Ceausescu pounded the table in defiance of the judges who tried him. Elena, his wife, broke down as she tried to add her protests. Soldiers bound the couple's hands for execution, but not their bodies. Within nine days of the first protest in Timisoara, this megalomaniacal despot and his wife, Elena, were hastily led outside to an open courtyard. Unceremoniously they were put in front of an army firing squad and executed. Their bullet-riddled bodies were put on display so that video evidence could be given to all Romanians and the world that Nicolae and Elena Ceausescu were dead. By the next morning, all resistance to the revolution in Romania ceased, and the shooting faded away.

The Securitate were put on the run. Many of them were arrested and put on public trial while others mysteriously disappeared. It is known that some of these former tormentors of society suffered revenge executions while others escaped arrest.

The National Salvation Front, made up of hastily combined political groups, faced many challenges to govern the liberated nation. The country was virtually bankrupt and they were aware that the transition from tyrannical dictatorship to democracy would not be easy. Nevertheless, Christians and church groups basked in their newfound liberties. For the first time in forty years they were free from constant harassment; they were allowed to travel beyond the borders of Romania, and they were free to receive foreign visitors such as Rev. Stanley Barnes and his colleagues.

When Pastor Eugen introduced the Free Presbyterian minister to share his testimony with the folk at the weekly prayer meeting and speak about his ministry in Ulster, Stanley felt overwhelmed. He counted himself unworthy to address this assembly of believers who had suffered so much for their Lord; however, Pastor Eugen explained to Stanley that for many years his people had been starved of fellowship from other Christians from abroad, and now they were anxious to hear how God was working in other lives and through other ministries.

Eugen spoke excellent English and acted as Stanley's interpreter when he greeted the congregation. The Free Presbyterian minister proceeded to share his testimony. By the time he had concluded the story of what God had done in his own life, he was not only overwhelmed by what the grace of God had done for him and in him but also that the Lord should give him the privilege to fellowship with this church in Timisoara at such a crucial and formative time in their history.

On that Wednesday night neither Stanley nor Eugen could have imagined the significance of that initial meeting or anticipated the consequences of the bond that was forged between these two pastors and their respective churches for years to come. However, God knew what was happening.

Chapter 2

Early Days

In 1942 Roslyn Street was one of a labyrinth of streets of terraced and red brick houses tightly compacted together between Belfast's Woodstock Road and the Ravenhill Road. While many other parts of the city had been devastated during the German blitz a year earlier, this working class area of Belfast had escaped the terror of those terrible air raids. Nevertheless, all families of that era suffered because of World War II. Food, clothes and energy were rationed; wages were low, and ordinary families had barely enough to meet their needs

The Barnes family lived in 13 Roslyn Street at the corner of Imperial Street. Although the spacious Ormeau Park was not too far away, Stanley and his seven brothers preferred to kick a football, spin a perrie with a whip or take advantage of the air-raid shelters nearby to play cowboys and Indians with their friends.

These children were oblivious of the German threats to their country and the war that was waging in Europe. Not even the rationing of food or clothing seemed to bother them. They were as happy as the day was long as they indulged in their fun and games, except when they had to attend the local school.

The nearby Roslyn Street Primary School never really played a favourite role in the lives of the young Barnes boys. As far as Stanley was concerned school was one of those unwanted and boring impositions of his boyhood days.

Sunday school was different. Across the road from their home was the Emmanuel Mission Hall where Mr. John Proctor was the missioner. Mr. Proctor became a legend in the immediate district. Everybody knew him, and he knew just about every family on the Woodstock Road. Many sought his counsel regarding domestic problems. Young couples consulted him about their marriage plans, and he always had wise advice for them. He identified with the elderly and infirm whom he visited regularly, and he was not afraid to put his hand into his pocket to help some needy families who were passing through hard times. Mr. Proctor not only knew everybody in the district, he always made time to speak with the boys and girls on the street. John Proctor was so well liked that the Roslyn Street Emmanuel Hall became commonly known as Proctor's Hall- a tribute to this warmhearted man of God.

Stanley, his brothers and their sister, faithfully attended the Tuesday evening Children's Meeting as well as the afternoon Sunday School at the hall. One of the favourite events on the calendar to which all the local children looked forward was the annual Sunday School excursion. It was a whole day's outing for parents and children and was just as well organised as any military manoeuvre. Thirteen buses were required to transport the children and their parents to the seaside resort of Ballywalter. Pastor Proctor boarded each bus to pray with the children before they departed. He repeated this same exercise at the end of the day prior to the buses returning to Belfast. His genuine and consistent godly influence gave great authenticity to the message he preached from the pulpit and was a radiant testimony to the Saviour Whom he served.

One of Mr. Proctor's co-workers was John Phillips who was married to

Mr. Proctor's sister. John was a faithful Christian and a very pleasant man. When he spoke some of his words seemed to whistle through his teeth, and this gave him a peculiar and unforgettable tone of voice. Besides being the Sunday School superintendent, John was also the leader of the Children's Meeting. He had an exceptional talent for teaching Bible verses and stories. Although young Stanley and his friends may not have been aware of it then, this godly man was sowing scriptural seeds into their young hearts which would blossom and flourish into a great spiritual harvest many years later.

John's weekly Bible teaching certainly created a reverence and fear of God in Stanley's young heart. This was reflected in an amusing incident, which occurred one Tuesday evening at the weekly Children's Meeting. At one stage of the meeting Mr. Phillips announced to all the children that it was time for them to give their collection. Instead of Stanley surrendering his penny for the collection, he mischievously placed a metal washer into the offering plate. Stanley thought that even though the coin-like washer had a hole at its centre no one would notice the difference.

When Stanley attended the Children's Meeting on the following week Mr. Phillips made an announcement just before taking up the usual offering. He lifted up his hand with the offending coin-like washer between his fingers, "Boys and girls," he said, "last week someone put this washer into the offering plate instead of a coin. I want you to know that this is God's offering. He sees us and knows the person who did it, and He does not want you to do that again."

Young Stanley was immediately stricken with guilt and a sudden fear that God was going to judge him there and then. He carried that haunting sense of guilt home with him thinking all the while that the Lord was going to send roars of thunder and flashes of lightning from heaven before he could reach his house. You can be sure Stanley never tried to fool Mr. Phillips again, nor did he place another washer into any offering plate again. He had learned his lesson.

There is a saying that "boys will be boys". In every generation young lads become more involved in mischievous pranks and the rough and tumble of life than most girls. Life for the lads may not be only rougher but often more risky. When Stanley was eleven years old he fell foul of a juvenile fracas when another young boy threw a brick at him. Unfortunately, Stanley was not quick enough to dodge the weighty projectile that struck him so forcefully on the hip that he immediately fell to the ground writhing in pain. Some lads rallied round to help their wounded and pain stricken friend back to his home.

Mrs. Barnes was horrified to see Stanley in such pain. Not long before this he had been admitted to the hospital with Mastoiditis. This infection had been one of the leading causes of death among children in the United Kingdom prior to the introduction of antibiotics. After an examination and Xray the doctor discovered an abnormality of the mastoid bone due to the infection. This resulted in immediate surgery and consequently, he was subjected to a prolonged course of antibiotics and closely observed during that time. Now that he was almost recovered from that fearful episode he was in trouble all over again.

The hip injury was much worse than they could have imagined. Stanley lost some movement in his leg. After examinations at the hospital the doctors concluded that the injury had resulted in young Stanley suffering from a paretic hip, a condition typified by a paralysis of motor functions of the leg.

As a result of this diagnosis Stanley was admitted to Belfast's Haypark Children's Hospital where he spent several months encased in plaster of Paris from his waist down. Although he did not enjoy school, Stanley certainly never thought that he would skip his lessons for so long in this way.

When he was finally discharged from hospital young Stanley spent the next three months confined to a wheel chair. After he was finally allowed to walk again, he had to wear a steel calliper on his injured leg for almost a year. Another consequence of this incident was that Stanley had lost much of his intermediate education. At the time of his injury he had just transferred from the Roslyn Street Primary School to Park Parade Secondary School, but as a result of his hospitalisation and subsequent rehabilitation he had lost almost two vital years of schooling.

Stanley was not concerned about the lost time in class. He was looking forward to his fourteenth birthday when he would be able to leave school for good and make his way in the world of employment.

When that fourteenth birthday arrived Stanley's formal schooling at Park Parade ended, but this young man still had a lot to learn.

Chapter 3

Conversion to Christ

Without any academic qualifications under his belt Stanley was limited in finding any pen-pushing or office employment. Furthermore, he was not particularly interested in any clerical positions. He much preferred to learn a skill in which he could use his hands and earn a decent wage.

While many of his local contemporaries went to learn a trade at Belfast's famed Harland and Wolff Shipyard or the Short's Aircraft factory, a different avenue of work opened for the teenage Stanley Barnes. He was recruited to be an apprentice baker at the nearby UCBS (United Cooperative Baking Society) on Ravenhill Avenue. Not only did the job seem to have good prospects, the bakery was less than half a mile from his home.

It did not take long for Stanley to become used to his new surroundings. He quickly made friends with his work colleagues. Before he knew it he was being drawn into company and habits that had been alien to him previously. Besides learning the tricks and skills of his bakery trade, Stanley was introduced to a round of lunch-hour card games. Very soon he found that he had become very adept at playing poker and was able to win a few coins in this way. In time poker almost became a lunchtime addiction for him.

With some money in his pocket Stanley was more able to indulge in other pleasurable pursuits. The Willowfield Picture House, better known locally as "The Winkie" and the Castle and the Ambassador cinemas became regular haunts. John Wayne was Stanley's favourite movie star, and he often remarked that he had become so addicted to this star of the silver screen that he was sure that John Wayne and his father must have won World War II between them.

Dancing and drinking alcohol quickly became another part of Stanley's social life. Like many other young men before him and since, he was misled into thinking that imbibing alcohol was what transformed a boy into becoming a macho man. Even though he had given up Sunday School and attendance at church services, Stanley could not escape from Christian influences or Christians. His sister, Winnie, the eldest in the family, had become a Christian and continued to attend the Emmanuel Mission Hall.

Besides Winnie's influence at home Stanley became acquainted with another Christian at work. Alec McAuley was a baker at the UCBS, and Stanley considered him to be a Christian gentleman. He never forced his religion on others, but he certainly walked the Christian walk and was not ashamed to speak of Jesus Christ when opportunity arose. Even though Stanley continued to be involved every day with the card-school fraternity, he respected Alec McAuley and all that he stood for.

One day Alec had a gentle rebuke for Stanley. On his way to a tea break, always having a weakness for apple-creams, Stanley picked up an unfinished pastry and apple from a tray. He took it over to Alec who was putting fresh cream on the pastries. "Put a dab of cream on that for me Alec," said Stanley.

Alec looked up at Stanley and said, "Stanley, I'm a Christian and those apple-creams don't belong to me or to you. I'm sorry, but I will not be putting cream on it for you."

Stanley was stunned. He hardly knew what to say, but after mumbling some sort of apology, he slank away with the apple and pastry still in his hand. He felt as if his conscience had shot an arrow of guilt straight into his heart. Nevertheless, he ate the apple and casing without the cream, but in doing so it seemed as though he had swallowed a lump of lead.

On another night in Ballyhackamore, East Belfast, he was having a drink in a bar with his brother before going to a dance at the nearby Brookeborough Hall on the Sandown Road. After Stanley had drained the last dregs from the tall glass of beer, he looked down into the bottom of the empty tumbler and watched the final bubbles of froth evaporate. He thought to himself, *That is exactly how my life is, empty and void. It counts for nothing.*

Stanley was still only a teenager, but he was dissatisfied and disillusioned; he felt his life was aimless and empty. Nevertheless, he continued on his way to the dance.

On a night not long after this incident, in May 1959, Stanley decided to go to see a movie at a cinema on the Woodstock Road. He called by the home of his friend, Jim Barnes (same surname but no relation). Jim's mother said that her son had already gone out. At that Stanley had a change of heart. He did not relish going to the cinema on his own.

It was then that Stanley remembered that his sister, Winnie, had invited him to attend one of the evangelistic meetings that were being conducted at the Emmanuel Mission Hall across the road from his home. Stanley later learned that they were being held to commemorate the Centenary Anniversary of the great 1859 Ulster Revival during which it was estimated that over 100,000 people had been converted.

For this special occasion Mr. Ernie Allen of the Revival Movement had arranged for the famed American evangelist and converted Jew, Dr. Hyman Appleman, and a team of American evangelists to visit Belfast to conduct a series of special evangelistic meetings. While Dr. Appleman conducted meetings in the Wellington Hall in Belfast's city centre, other evangelistic campaigns were organised throughout the city.

One of Dr. Appleman's evangelistic team was a young Texan, Johnny Bisango. Before his conversion Johnny had been the leader of a popular dance band and a solo trumpet and trombone player of some renown in his native USA. Now as an evangelist, he used his musical talents for the glory of God. Johnny was invited to conduct special evangelistic meetings at the Emmanuel Mission Hall.

In anticipation of the Johnny Bisango's visit Pastor Proctor and his friends at the Roslyn Street Emmanuel Mission Hall worked hard. They visited every home in the Woodstock and Cregagh Road areas to invite people to attend the special meetings.

Winnie, zealous to win her family for the Lord, had invited Stanley on several occasions to attend the mission. Without Jim Barnes' company to go with him to the cinema, Stanley was left at a loose end. He decided this would be the right opportunity to satisfy Winnie and go to hear this American dance bandleader at the Emmanuel Hall.

Stanley had already heard of other people being converted at the meetings, but he was convinced it would never happen to him. Although he would not be disrespectful of Christians, he was really not too interested in religion. He intended to sit at the rear of the small hall, and as soon as the meeting finished he would slip out again.

Stanley was surprised to see that the Roslyn Street hall was packed with people of all ages. The meeting was bright and the singing was enthusiastic. As had been announced, Johnny Bisango played various trumpet solos and Stanley was very impressed.

Initially, when the evangelist began to preach Stanley's attention was held by the young evangelist's Texas drawl; however, as he continued to listen he became even more arrested by what the evangelist was saying. Johnny Bisango spoke of the love of God as expressed in the sufferings of Jesus Christ on Calvary's cross. Since he had been a young boy Stanley had known about the crucifixion of Jesus Christ, but on that night it seemed so personal and individual. Johnny Bisango explained from the pulpit that God's love was so great for each person that Christ had died for the individual. Stanley was overwhelmed at this.

When the preacher finished delivering his passionate message he asked for all of the congregation to bow their heads and reverently sing the invitation hymn:

> Just as I am, without one plea,
> But that Thy blood was shed for me,
> And that Thou bidst me come to thee,
> O Lamb of God, I come, I come.

> Just as I am, thy love unknown
> Hath broken every barrier down;
> Now, to be Thine, yea Thine alone,
> O Lamb of God, I come, I come.

All the barriers that Stanley had previously imagined would prevent him from becoming a Christian, were inexplicably broken down. There was no more resistance in his heart. During the singing of the first verse of the hymn, Stanley rose from his seat at the rear of the hall and unashamedly went to the front to indicate his decision to trust Jesus Christ as his Saviour.

After the people finished singing, John Phillips, the man Stanley had earlier known as the leader of the Children's Meeting and his Sunday School teacher, led him to the enquiry room. There the two of them knelt beside one of the old forms that Stanley had sat on during his Sunday School days. John asked him to read John 3:16; "For God so loved the world, that he gave his only begotten Son, that whosoever believeth in him should not perish, but have everlasting life."

John invited Stanley to substitute some words with his own name to read as follows; "For God so loved *Stanley Barnes*, that he gave his only begotten Son, that if *Stanley Barnes* believeth in him he should not perish, but *Stanley Barnes* should have everlasting life." This confirmed to Stanley just what he had heard from the preacher in the meeting, that God's love for him was personal and individual.

John then asked Stanley to make a personal prayer to God, confess his sin, ask God to forgive him and come into his heart. Stanley followed these steps and sincerely asked the Lord Jesus to save him.

There was great joy after the meeting when Mr. Proctor and the evangelist shook Stanley's hand and encouraged him to wholly follow the Lord. His sister, Winnie, wept with joy for her brother's conversion was an answer to her prayers.

Stanley would still need his sister's prayers. He would have to tell his friends and colleagues at work of this radical step he had taken. He knew that would not be easy. However, Mr. Proctor assured him that God had never promised that the Christian life would be easy, but the Lord had promised to always be with him and give him the strength he needed.

Chapter 4

A New Beginning

When Stanley told his friends at the UCBS Bakery that he had become a Christian some gave him two weeks before he would be back to the card school and his old ways. Others like Alec McAuley, who later became a Methodist minister, were delighted with Stanley's news and encouraged him to keep going on. He was glad he was never going back to his old way of life. He proved that the God who kept Daniel in the den of lions in Babylon so long ago was able to keep him in the UCBS Bakery and elsewhere.

Stanley did not miss a night of the remaining meetings at the Emmanuel Mission Hall. Johnny Bisango had never conducted evangelistic meetings prior to this. His main contribution to Christian work until then had always been expressed through his musical talents. As a result of the success of the special meetings at the Emmanuel Mission Johnny was constrained to enter into pastoral ministry. He eventually became pastor of the First Baptist Church of Houston, Texas and was later elected to be the President of the Southern Baptist Convention.

When the centenary meetings had finished Stanley continued to attend the Emmanuel Hall. Stanley enjoyed the convenience of living across the road from the hall; he gleaned tremendous help from Pastor Proctor's preaching and Bible teaching ministry in those early days of his Christian life.

The famed Bible teacher, Graham Scroggie, once said, "Too many Christians live on the right side of Easter, but on the wrong side of Pentecost, the right side of pardon, but on the wrong side of power, the right side of forgiveness, but on the wrong side of fellowship. They are out of Egypt, but have not reached the land of promise and blessing. They are still wandering about in the wilderness of frustration and dissatisfaction."

As a new convert Stanley Barnes did not want to remain stagnant or drift away from the first steps he had taken as a Christian. Right from the first weeks of his new-found life in Christ he wanted to know more of the Bible and to grow spiritually and to be effective for God. Having had his spiritual appetite stimulated through Pastor Proctor's Bible ministry he wanted to reach for the very best in his Christian life.

In those early years of his Christian experience Stanley was nurtured further when he came under the influence and ministry of various men and women of God. He was challenged through the preaching of Rev. Bert Cooke of Mount Merrion Free Presbyterian Church and by Dr. Ian Paisley's powerful preaching at the Ravenhill Free Presbyterian Church who was making a great impact on Belfast and beyond. Stanley not only warmed to Dr. Paisley's preaching, it was at the Ravenhill church that he was also greatly blessed when Pastor Willie Mullen was invited to conduct a series of Bible studies there.

The annual Easter Convention at the Ravenhill Church was another highpoint of the year. Guest speakers such as Mary Morrison gave a first hand account of the revival on her native Isle of Lewis in the mid-1950s. Bob and Alma McAllister, returning missionaries from Congo with UFM, spoke with great passion and challenge of the spiritual revival in the heart of Africa. Willie Weir, a former missionary in India, never ceased to bless the congregation as he related his burden for God's work through the Worldwide Evangelisation Crusade (WEC). Jordan Khan, a forthright and authoritative preacher from India, stirred the people as he preached on revival night after night. Ernie Allen, founder of the Revival Movement and the Every Home Crusade was a quiet spoken man, but he spoke passionately of his tremendous burden for a worldwide ministry through literature.

These servants of God left a mighty imprint on Stanley's heart and life. Furthermore, Dr. Paisley's weekly ministry convinced him that he should make Ravenhill Free Presbyterian Church his spiritual home. Thereafter, Stanley committed himself to be involved in the weekly programme of church activities.

At the same time as he was growing spiritually, Stanley felt he also needed some physical recreation. After all, he was still a teenager and having suffered a prolonged illness a few years earlier, he wanted to build up his physical stamina. Not too far away from where Stanley lived, a young George Best from the Cregagh was honing his soccer skills at a local boys' club. Like George, Northern Ireland's greatest ever soccer player, most young men wanted to kick a football or play rugby. Stanley, however, indulged in an even more aggressive activity. He joined a local judo club in Belfast and was soon learning all the moves and skills of this martial art. He not only enjoyed the energetic expertise and techniques of throwing his opponents to the mat, he also became accomplished at how to fall to the floor without breaking any bones.

With the frequent rough and tumble of the judo exercises Stanley began to make steady progress in developing his judo skills. To attain to the level of expertise he desired meant that he had to give more time and diligence to these training exercises. Within time he was attending the judo club five nights each week and was there again for several hours every Saturday afternoon. During his lunch hour at the UCBS he tied bags of flour to a pillar and proceeded to kick at the bag as he tried to sharpen his speed at various judo moves and technics. With this persistence Stanley developed great adaptability and was soon ambidextrous in combatting his opponents with his hands and feet.

His continued practice sessions helped Stanley advance through the different stages. First, he gained the White belt and then proceeded to the Yellow. This was followed by success to gain the Orange, Green, Blue and Brown belts. His aspiration was to attain to the highest qualification which was the Black Belt. By this time Stanley's keenness for this martial-art activity had just about taken over his life. It seemed that every hour outside employment or church on Sunday, he was eating and sleeping judo.

Just as he neared the pinnacle of his development at the martial-art club Stanley fell ill again. At first he felt he was too weak to go to work. Later he developed such a high fever that his mother called the doctor. After examining Stanley carefully, the doctor took a little while before he turned to the anxious mother and said, "Mrs. Barnes, your son is very ill. I think he has either got meningitis or polio. We will have to get him to the hospital immediately."

Stanley was admitted to Belfast City Hospital and for some days it seemed as if he was hovering on the brink of eternity. The medical staff administered intramuscular and intravenous injections every four hours until the fever began to recede and Stanley's condition stabilised. He remained in hospital for several weeks to recover from the perilous episode.

During this time of convalescence Stanley had time to reflect on his life and his close encounter with death. He concluded that as a Christian he was not afraid to die, but at the same time, he would have been ashamed to die. He felt that he had not been all that he should have been as a Christian and had done very little in his life for the Kingdom of God.

One day while Stanley was still in hospital, he received a pastoral visit from the Rev. S. B, Cooke. In conversation with the pastor he shared these anxious thoughts. The Rev. Cooke indicated to Stanley the importance of Christian priorities as expressed in Matthew 6:33; "But seek ye first the kingdom of God, and his righteousness; and all these things shall be added unto you."

Stanley confessed that his dedication to judo had subtly taken over his life and had slowly suffocated his Christian zeal. The pastor told Stanley that the Lord could raise him up again and make his life useful for God. After the minister prayed, Stanley also called upon God and rededicated his life to the Lord. The Rev. Cooke knew that this was a big step for the young man. There and then and without any hesitation, Stanley decided to give up his judo training.

That visit from Rev. Cooke turned out to be a pivotal moment in Stanley's life. When he returned home to Roslyn Street and to a form of normality, his appetite for spiritual things was reinvigorated. But while he had been impressed and challenged by a succession of missionaries who had spoken at the annual Easter Convention, Stanley thought that there was no way he could ever serve God as these great men and women of God had done. At the same time he did not want to recoil from anything that God might want him to do. He wrestled in his heart a conflicting sense of his personal inadequacy and inferiority against a feeling of accountability and commitment to the will of God. He wondered if these contradictory attitudes could be reconciled in his life.

The answer to Stanley's musings came one Sunday morning when Dr. Ian Paisley preached on Psalm 78:9; "The children of Ephraim, being armed, and carrying bows, turned back in the day of battle." The preacher pointed out that the children of Ephraim were the largest and most prominent of the tribes in Israel and were adequately equipped for the Lord's battle. However, they failed to fulfil their potential and retreated from their obligations to God and Israel.

In the course of his message Dr. Paisley leaned over the pulpit and called out, "Young man, will God write over the story of your life that you turned back in the day of battle, or will you go through with Him?"

These words resounded in Stanley's heart and answered the conflict with which he had been wrestling. He sensed that God was clearly calling him into Christian ministry. At the end of that Sunday morning service he quietly surrendered his will to the will of God.

Later that night he pondered in his mind and heart, If God is calling me, what is the next step?

Chapter 5

Student Days at MTC

During 1964 news began to filter through to the outside world of the terrible atrocities that were happening in the heart of Africa. The Simba (Lion) rebels in eastern Congo were locked in savage battles with government soldiers and were quickly advancing across the country from east to west. In their wake they left a trail of gory massacres in which thousands of people were butchered, women raped and villages pillaged. The undisciplined ragtag army of Simba rebels executed thousands of people, including government officials, political leaders of the opposition parties, police officers, teachers and other Congolese suspected to have been westernised. Many of these executions were carried out with bloody and extreme savagery.

Missionaries of all denominations were not spared this cruel scourge of senseless carnage. Many of them were lined up before firing squads and executed in cold blood. Others like Denis Parry, who was a college colleague of Dr. Paisley, his wife Nora and their two children, Ruby Gray from Dromara, County Down, and her medical colleagues Dr. Ian and Audrey Sharp and their three children, were all gunned down and their bodies thrown to the crocodiles in the River Congo. These are only a few of the Lord's noble Christian soldiers who were so ruthlessly massacred for the gospel.

Belfast missionaries, Bob and Alma McAllister, were held captive but were liberated by mercenary soldiers as were Jim and Ida Grainger who belonged to the Welcome Hall in Belfast. Dr. Helen Roseveare suffered horrifically in captivity, and many of her colleagues were held captive for a prolonged period before being brutally executed. WEC missionaries Bill McChesney, who was only twenty-eight years old, and Jim Rodgers, his Scottish colleague, after days of torture, were mercilessly beaten to death with clubs, kicks, trampling and fists.

The alarming news updates that continued to shock the world were not only sorrowful, they were also sobering for a young man like Stanley Barnes who was contemplating stepping out to serve God as a missionary. At the same time Stanley had become acquainted with the famous and stirring motto of the founder of WEC, Charles C. Studd: "If Jesus Christ be God and died for me, then no sacrifice can be too great for me to make for Him."

Of this motto, the young martyr, Bill McChesney, wrote:

> If He be God, and died for me, no sacrifice too great can be
> For me, a mortal man, to make; I'll do it all for Jesus' sake.
> Yes, I will tread the path He trod; no other way will please my God;
> So, henceforth, this my choice shall be, my choice for all eternity.

Undeterred by the horrendous sufferings and sacrifice of so many of these Christian stalwarts, Stanley still pursued God's will for his life whatever might be the cost. He shared with Dr. Paisley how God had been speaking to him about Christian service with a view to missionary work abroad and asked for his counsel. The pastor encouraged him to trust God for guidance in each step. He also recommended to Stanley that he consider following several other missionaries from the church who had trained at the Worldwide Evangelisation Crusade Missionary Training College (MTC) in Glasgow.

When Stanley arrived at the MTC at the beginning of October 1964 he looked at the sign which arched above the front gate of the college:

"Have Faith in God". How appropriate these words were for him. He would need to be trusting in the Lord to help him through his studies. When he had left Park Parade School he thought it had been the happiest day of his life. Never in his wildest dreams did he think that he would ever be back behind a school desk to cope with lots of studies and assignments.

On arrival in Glasgow he discovered he was not alone in being apprehensive about having to return to studies. Other students were not only in the same boat, they also had arrived at MTC with the same commitment and aspiration - to prepare for the Lord's service wherever that might be. Victor Cardoo from Great Victoria Street Baptist Church, Desmond Branagh from Newtownbreda Baptist and Norman Gray from the Templemore Hall all commenced their studies at MTC at the same time as Stanley. He quickly made good friends with these and other students with whom he would be living in close proximity for the next two years.

At MTC Stanley rapidly discovered that this course did not only involve studying the scriptures. He had to relearn the basics of English grammar in order to be able to write the college dissertations. How he wished he had paid more attention to the English lessons years earlier at the Park Parade School. Stanley is still not sure if the English classes were a greater challenge to the resident English teacher, Miss Rachael McDonald, or to himself. When asked to name the various types of nouns Stanley did not have a clue so he answered, "I am not sure, but I know there are low downs, go downs and show downs." Other students laughed at his comical answer, but Miss McDonald was less than impressed and gave Stanley a deserved dressing down in front of the whole class.

However, having to learn the basics of English grammar and read widely ultimately worked for Stanley's good. It created in him an insatiable desire for literature and started him on a pathway in which his acquaintance with books would become a major part of his future ministry. He was an avid and quick reader with a great capacity to retain what he had read, an enviable aptitude for anyone in Christian ministry.

Before travelling to MTC Stanley was not aware that the college had an excellent library. In his ignorance he brought dozens of commentaries and reference books to college to help with his studies. When he arrived one of the staff wanted to know what he had in his cases and why they were so heavy. Stanley was a little embarrassed and deferred in answering.

MTC was designed to furnish the students with a good comprehensive knowledge of the scriptures and the fundamentals of theology. The course also put great emphasis on character building, creating vision, initiative and passion for God's work around the world and equipping the students with skills that would make them effective servants of God. All of the staff at MTC had an accumulative wealth of missionary experience that qualified them for their work.

Some months after Stanley's arrival at MTC the Director of Studies, Bill Chapman and his wife Moira, took leave of absence to take up a similar post in Ghana, West Africa. Roy and Daphne Spragget, former WEC missionaries in Vietnam, stepped in to take over their leadership role. Roy had been injured in a shell explosion in Vietnam and this led to their premature return to United Kingdom. Bill and Peggy Easton, who had spent many years in Columbia, assisted Roy and Daphne. They also had suffered greatly during the persecution that prevailed in that Latin American country at that time. Both of these couples made a great impression on all the students and Stanley maintains that he owes much to their godly example of sacrifice and dedication.

Mr. and Mrs. Fran Rowbotham were affectionately known to all in WEC as Pa and Ma Rowe. They were the founders of MTC and were also WEC leaders in Scotland. They were the embodiment of faith, sacrifice, holiness and fellowship - the four pillars of the WEC. Pa Rowe was an energetic servant of God who was always reaching for bigger and greater things with giant steps of faith. Ma Rowe was also a woman of faith and great wisdom but in a more reserved, devotional and discerning manner. When she spoke people listened and learned much from her godly counsel. The students used to remark that Ma and Pa Rowe might have been nicknamed "Faith and Works" because of their contrasting and complementary qualities. Stanley counted it a great blessing to have had the benefit and example of such godly leaders during those formative years.

Along with studies in the classroom the MTC students engaged in other activities outside the college. On Sunday afternoons they held open-air meetings at the famous Glasgow Barrowland Market, commonly known as "The Barras".

At the weekends they were often sent out to testify and preach in churches and mission halls in and around Glasgow. When free, Stanley and his college friends loved to attend the Saturday Night Rallies at the Tent Hall when Dr. Stanley Collins gave great expositions of the Word of God. The college staff organised quarterly missionary conferences at MTC when challenges were presented from visiting missionaries. Besides the weekly "WEC Prayer Battery" on Friday evenings there were also days of prayer and fasting.

Mission teams of college students were sent to various parts of Scotland for two weeks in April each year. The first mission team Stanley took part in was to a Baptist church in Kirkwall, the capital of the Orkney Isles. God blessed those two weeks of meetings. God's people were blessed and several people trusted in the Lord Jesus Christ. During his final year Stanley led a mission team to a small Brethren Hall in Kilwinning, Ayrshire. This again was an enriching experience for him and a blessing to the local assembly.

Stanley enjoyed the welcome breaks at Christmas and Easter when he was able to go home to visit his family and friends at Ravenhill Free Presbyterian Church which faithfully supported him throughout his training years. However, most of the long summer holidays were spent at Kilcreggan, the WEC holiday home on the northern shore of the Firth of Clyde. During those vacation weeks visiting WEC missionaries addressed the gatherings and spoke passionately of their work in different countries. Hundreds of people from all over the United Kingdom and beyond enjoyed great hospitality and the meetings morning and evening. Len Moules, the International Secretary of WEC and a highly respected missionary statesman, challenged and enriched the visitors by his daily Bible readings.

Needless to say, it was not possible to have some sixty young students living in close proximity for two years without some shenanigans or horseplay taking place, especially when several of them were from Northern Ireland. Stanley Barnes, who always had a quick sense of humour, and Dessie Branagh, who was a born comedian, were the worst culprits for this mischievous behaviour. By the time these two students had completed their two-year course at Glasgow the MTC staff were grateful to have retained their sanity.

Graduation from MTC in June 1966 meant Stanley would be leaving Glasgow, but he was taking with him many happy memories, and not only memories, but godly and lasting imprints that had been made on his life.

He was ready to go anywhere the Lord might lead him, but where would that be?

Chapter 6

A Change of Direction

Near the end of the 1966 summer season at Kilcreggan Stanley and another student got up to another one of their pranks. They decided to hide in some bushes at the side of a road on the holiday home grounds. Their plan was to jump out on a visiting and unsuspecting family known to them and give them a fright. From their hiding place they could hear the increasing chatter of holiday makers approaching. Judging that these were their unwary victims, the two boys crouched down ready to pounce out from behind the bush. When they suddenly pounced out with accompanying loud yells it did startle the people, but it was too late to realise they had made a mistake. These individuals were not their intended target. They had mistakenly jumped out on three WEC leaders and this was just at the time Stanley was making application to the mission. Embarrassment is a light word to describe how these two pranksters and would-be missionaries felt. Although the leaders were startled they soon gave the boys a fool's pardon and went on their way.

Stanley was relieved to learn that his ill-timed and mischievous prank at Kilcreggan did not hinder him from being accepted for the WEC Candidates Course at the mission headquarters in Upper Norwood, London. He had given a lot of thought and prayer to where the Lord might be leading him. Tom and Lily McClelland, Bill Woods, and Victor and Audrey Maxwell, all members of the Free Presbyterian Church, were already serving God in Brazil, and this had made some constraint on Stanley. At that time WEC were developing a new ministry in Brazil, and several missionaries from the United Kingdom and Holland were already working in the Brazilian state of Minas Gerais. Stanley initially thought that might be where the Lord was leading him and had therefore applied to WEC for service in South America.

Stanley found the Candidates Course to be a little more relaxed than the strict disciplines at MTC. Besides learning about comparative religions, foreign cultures and phonetics, there were extended seasons of prayer for the situation in the heart of Africa. Since the Simba rebellion in Congo in 1964 dozens of Christian missionaries had been martyred, imprisoned or abused, including many of the WEC personnel. Other missionaries were yet unaccounted for and while they were still missing the mission leadership called for special times of prayer for them. Those were solemn and tearful seasons of prayer and intercession.

One of the most powerful and impressionable experiences for Stanley and the other students was the moving account given of the Memorial Service for the missionaries of several missionary societies who had been martyred in the Congo. It was held in Dr. Martin Lloyd Jones' Westminster Chapel. Besides the Chapel being filled to capacity with 3,000 people, the Institute Hall and the Intermediate Hall were also full, and crowds of people who were not able to gain admittance waited on the street outside.

The service was conducted by Rev. Gilbert Kirby. After the great congregation sang the hymn A Safe Stronghold our God is Still and the opening prayer, four missionaries from Congo testified of their gruesome experiences and God's deliverance during the Congo rebellion. There were very few dry eyes as these harrowing reports were given.

During the Act of Remembrance, which was led by Rev. Leonard Harris of UFM, the names of those who had given their lives for Christ and others who were still missing and presumed dead, were read out: "A Noble Army of Christian Martyrs," of whom the world was not worthy. Remembrance was also made of thousands of Congolese Christians and church leaders who had also been massacred during those terrible days in Africa. Stanley was not alone when he was moved to tears as the names were poignantly read out one after another.

The climax of the service came when Len Moules gave the final address. He based his memorial message on 1 Peter 1:6, the verse which Muriel Harman, one of the WEC martyrs, gave to her fellow missionaries in captivity while blood was trickling down her face after being been beaten with truncheons: "Wherein ye greatly rejoice, though now for a season, if need be, ye are in heaviness through manifold temptations." She admonished them from Philips' translation, "Even though at present you are temporarily harassed by all kinds of trials and temptations this is no accident – it happens to prove your faith."

Len Moules said to the packed church, "This was her anchorage when driven into the death room to be machine-gunned down with many others."

With the obvious anointing of God on him, Len went on to speak of the atrocities in the light of this verse:

1. It was a proving of their faith to the glory of God (1 Peter 1:6).
2. It was a pruning for fruit to the glory of God (John 15:2).
3. It was promoting the return in glory of the Son of God (Revelation 6:11).

At the conclusion of his message Len Moules challenged the massive crowd:

Congo has made her deposit in the vaults of heaven, yet there is still a balance to be paid - the price of the unfinished task. The challenge of today is as real and vital as yesterday. We have the equipment, the science and engineering to do the job in this generation, but the price must be paid.

Stanley was greatly stirred by what he heard. He could do no more than yield his life afresh to God for whatever His will might entail in the future. Another poem written by the young WEC martyr, Bill McChesney, revealed his highest motives and reflected how Stanley felt in that dedicatory moment:

> He left His glory-circled throne
> Midst heaven's purest light,
> To make this world His fleshly home,
> A world of sin and night.
>
> He left it all, not seeking crown,
> Nor diadem so fair,
> But seeking men by sin cast down
> And sunken in despair.
>
> If He be God and died for me,
> To take away my sin,
> No sacrifice too great can be
> For me to make for Him.

In the course of his time at the London headquarters Stanley was still aiming to go to Brazil. After consideration of his medical history of mastoiditis and a paretic hip, the mission's leadership thought it advisable for him to have a medical at the London Tropical Hospital. Stanley did not contemplate there would be any problem in subjecting himself to a medical, for he felt he enjoyed good health.

The doctor who examined him was familiar with all the procedure of the WEC in relation to their missionary candidates. He had examined many prospective missionaries before meeting Stanley Barnes. The doctor listened carefully to him tell of his past illnesses when he was a boy. After a physical examination the doctor told him that with his history of mastoiditis he could not recommend him to live in the tropics in case he should have a recurrence of the infection.

Stanley was shocked. He never thought there was any reason why he would not be able to face the rigours of a tropical climate. Nevertheless, the WEC Candidates Committee confirmed to him what the doctor had advised them; therefore, they were not able to accept him for the WEC work in Brazil.

At first Stanley felt his plans had been shattered. He believed that God had been leading him to this place and in due time would open the door to Brazil with WEC, but now the door had been firmly closed in his face. How could this be? he wondered.

It was while he was mulling this over and praying before the Lord about his thwarted plans that he remembered the theme Len Moules had preached on at the Martyrs' Memorial Service – "This is no Accident". True faith must be tried faith. Since coming into training at MTC he had learned much about the life of faith. Len Moules had stressed that the secular world demands the stamp of test and quality; bridges have their load factors, and jewellery has its hallmark. So also, the servant of God must bear the imprint of a faith that has been tried and survived the trial.

Stanley packed his belongings to move back to Northern Ireland, a little disappointed that he was not able to follow through on the plans he had been previously sure about. Although he was going back to Belfast he did not know what he was going to do in the immediate future. Dr. Paisley had always been a wise counsellor for Stanley when he had faced other crises in his Christian life. Perhaps he would be able to help again.

"Brother Stanley," said the supportive Dr. Paisley, "The Lord has a plan in this. Don't go back into secular employment. There are openings for you here. I suggest you should apply to the Presbytery to be accepted as a student at the Theological Hall and consider entering the ministry."

Was this the next step?

Chapter 7

In Transition

The dozens of volumes of theological books that Stanley had transported to Glasgow, had to be transferred back to Belfast. He certainly would need them when he embarked on another four years of studies at the Free Presbyterian Theological Hall. At these classes he was accompanied by other students who would become his future colleagues in the ministry of the Free Church - Frank McClelland, Michael Patrick, William McCrea, Ivan Foster, Gordon Cooke, John Long and Fred Greenfield.

His tutors at the Hall deepened and enriched his love for the scriptures and enhanced his flair for preaching the Word of God. Dr. Paisley was Professor of Church History, and his love for the Reformation and the great spiritual revivals of former years was very much in evidence as he lectured. Rev. John Douglas, Professor of English Bible, led his students through the scriptures book by book. Rev. S. B. Cooke was Professor of Homiletics and Pastoral Theology and Rev. Alan Cairns was Professor of Theology. The contributions and influence of these men of God helped to shape the lives and ministry of their students for future years, but when all is said and done, the words of John Newton were very relevant for Stanley, "Only He who created the world is able also to make a true minister of the Gospel."

During these years Stanley became engrossed in his studies and thereby developed an even deeper love and attachment to his books. As bees taking the nectar from summer blossoms and producing wholesome honey, so Stanley delved into all sorts of books and gleaned from them. He read and imbibed theological classics, commentaries of the great divines, sermons of famous preachers from all eras and the biographies of great servants of God. These books were like rungs on a ladder by which this student minister was able to increase his knowledge of the Bible, appreciate deeper theological truths and appropriate the lessons he learned.

Beyond his new series of studies, Stanley was also invited to preach at various Free Presbyterian churches. Consequently, the session of Mount Merrion Free Presbyterian Church in Belfast requested at Presbytery that Stanley would be placed at their church as a student minister.

Stanley began his ministry at Mount Merrion on 6th January 1967, and he remained there for the next five years. During this, his first pastoral responsibility, he was able to hone his preaching skills and develop a warm relationship with those for whom he had pastoral care. It was also there that he gained considerable experience in how to handle difficult situations and help people in their problems.

While at Mount Merrion, Stanley gained more than experience; it was there that he began to pay special attention to one of the Sunday School teachers, Miss Ina Keefe. Ina had attended the church since she was a young girl, and one Sunday following the Sunday School lesson, her teacher, Joan Smylie, led Ina to faith in Jesus Christ.

After her conversion to Jesus Christ, Mount Merrion Free Presbyterian Church became Ina's spiritual home. In time she became part of the church's Youth Fellowship and was delighted when she was invited to teach in a Sunday School class.

Very soon Stanley and Ina were going out together. Two and a half years after his arrival at the church the happy couple were married at Mount Merrion Free Presbyterian Church on 2nd August 1969. The former minister of the Church, Rev. S. B. Cooke, officiated at the wedding ceremony.

Their unforgettable wedding day lives on in their memory for other reasons. That day also corresponded with the beginning of the outbreak of violence on Belfast's Crumlin Road. When Dr. Paisley was en route to the reception, his car was stoned as they passed by the Cromac Square district of the city.

During the ensuing week scores of houses in North Belfast were burned; hundreds of families were displaced; this was the beginning of an era in Ulster known as "The Troubles" which would last for the next thirty years.

Although Northern Ireland was unsettled, there was no trouble for the newly-weds. They sped off to London for their honeymoon and returned to occupy the manse, which was on an elevated site above Belfast city on the Castlereagh hills. From that vantage point they could see the fires of discontent and violence burning night after night all over the city. It seemed like Belfast was a cauldron of hostility as wars raged throughout the city.

In that tense atmosphere Stanley continued to apply himself to the ministry God had given him, preaching the Word from the pulpit, caring for the congregation and zealously sharing the Gospel to win the lost for Christ.

Having completed his studies at the Free Presbyterian Church Theological Hall in 1970, Stanley was ordained to the ministry of the church on the 17th December of that same year. Although he and Ina were well settled in the ministry at Mount Merrion he still had a persistent conviction that God was calling them to be missionaries. Despite having failed a medical to work in a tropical country, Stanley felt that the Lord was opening a door for them in Spain. Ina was more than content to follow where her husband felt the Lord was leading them. By this time the Lord had blessed their family with a precious daughter, Heather. In many ways it would have been easier for the young couple and their newborn child to remain in Belfast, but Stanley felt he had committed himself to go where God was leading him, and he would not shrink from the challenge.

Norman Gray, a fellow-student with Stanley at MTC in Glasgow, was working in Santander in Northern Spain and had shared with him the great need for a church-planting ministry in that region. Sensing that Santander was where the Lord was leading them, Stanley shared his sentiments with his ministerial colleagues and then with the Presbytery. Respecting God's call on his life and Ina's willingness to accompany her husband, the ministers and elders of the Presbytery agreed to send the young couple to Spain under the auspices of the Free Presbyterian Missionary Council.

After a series of deputation meetings around the increasing number of Free Presbyterian churches, Stanley and Ina and their little daughter said farewell to Ulster in March 1972 and left for Northern Spain. His period there turned out to be a particularly trying one. It soon became obvious that the time for the Free Presbyterian Church's mission to Spain had not yet come. As a result, Stanley and family had to return to Northern Ireland sooner than they had expected. At the time it was a big disappointment for Stanley and Ina, but they would subsequently learn that the Lord had other plans for the Free Presbyterian Church's incursion into Spain. This was not the Lord's time for them.

Although the term in Spain was short, it did give an added dimension to Stanley's future pastoral ministry in the Free Presbyterian Church. Because of their time on the Iberian Peninsula he not only continued to maintain a keen interest in missions but also a vital understanding of the various problems missionaries face.

Dr. Paisley was very understanding and benevolent for the young family on their return to Ulster. He told Stanley that there were many vacant churches in the denomination and there was no doubt the Lord had a plan for them. Stanley was heartened when he remembered

Len Moules' theme at Westminster Chapel, "This is no accident." God has His sovereign plan, and He was working out the future for the Barnes family.

Through the late 1960s and early 1970s there was rapid growth in the number of Free Presbyterian churches. Stanley was invited to help in visitation and preaching at three vacant congregations: Kilkeel, Larne and Hillsborough. This was an opportunity for these churches to consider inviting this young man to be their pastor. It was also an opportunity for him to consider God's guidance in his life.

The office-bearers at Hillsborough Free Presbyterian Church remembered the first time Stanley preached for them in 1967 when the church was meeting in a small and portable band hall. David Williamson, Clerk of Session of the church for more than three decades, recalled how they were struck with the strong impression Stanley's ministry had made on them. They were especially enthused about how he took time to address the children.

Those early impressions were not lost on the elders of the Hillsborough church who seized the opportunity to call Stanley to be their new minister. It did not take long for Stanley to ascertain that this was God's guidance and after a short period he accepted the church's invitation.

This was God's guidance indeed. Stanley was ordained as the minister of the Hillsborough Free Presbyterian Church in October 1972.

The close bond forged between pastor and congregation at Hillsborough was most certainly very secure, for Stanley and Ina remained in their role for the next thirty-five years.

Chapter 8

Foundations and Fruit

The Hillsborough Free Presbyterian Church had its beginnings in the midst of Ulster's turbulent political and religious agitations of the 1960s. During that decade three Free Presbyterian ministers, Dr. Ian Paisley, Rev. John Wylie and Rev. Ivan Foster, were charged and found guilty of a disturbance of the peace during a protest against the ecumenical trends of the Presbyterian Church in Ireland. When they refused to pay the fines levied against them or accept the terms of the bail bonds imposed by the court, they were incarcerated for three months. While they were imprisoned many of their fellow ministers criss-crossed Northern Ireland on a series of evangelistic campaigns in tents, Orange Halls and mission halls. Subsequently, many new Free Presbyterian congregations were founded

In the summer of 1966 the Rev. William Beattie, minister of Dunmurry Free Presbyterian Church, conducted one of these campaigns on the outskirts of the picturesque and historic village of Hillsborough. Several members of his Dunmurry congregation, namely James McCann and David Williamson, resided in the Hillsborough area and were keen to establish a strong Free Presbyterian witness in their district. They, therefore, invited Mr. Beattie to conduct a tent mission in their village.

Initially, Rev. Beattie and these men encountered considerable opposition in trying to secure a site for a Gospel mission in the village, but they were undeterred in their endeavours. Finally, the minister obtained permission from Mr. James Anderson to erect a tent in a field on his property, less than a mile outside the village.

These meetings were a great success, and on many nights the crowds attending had to sit on bales of straw outside the tent. Better still, many people were converted during those weeks of Gospel preaching. Much to David Williamson's delight, five members of his family trusted Christ as Saviour and James McCann was also blessed with the good news that his uncle and aunt had become Christians at the special meetings.

After the final tent meeting about twenty people asked to have a meeting with Rev. William Beattie at which they expressed their desire to help form a Free Presbyterian Church in the Hillsborough district. Their biggest problem was to find a suitable place where they could conduct the meetings. Mr. and Mrs. Matt Spratt, neighbours of James Anderson who had been converted at the tent meetings, were more than willing to allow the fledging congregation to congregate in their barn. However, the ever-enthusiastic James McCann gained permission for the first congregational meetings to be held in the Edenticullo Band Hall not far from the village and on the Ballynahinch Road.

The first worship service took place at the Band Hall on Sunday, 4th September 1966. That initial meeting was crowned by two more people trusting in Jesus Christ as Saviour. Later that week, 9th September 1966, a small group of these Christians submitted a petition to the Presbytery asking for them to be formed into a Free Presbyterian Church. The ministers and elders at the Presbytery had great pleasure to accede to their request and accordingly, the Hillsborough Free Presbyterian Church was born.

The new congregation remained at Edenticullo Band Hall until March 1968. After that the church leadership decided to erect a portable hall on a half-acre of land rented from Mr. Matt Spratt on Hillsborough's Comber Road. Although building permission was not normally required in the 1960s for portable or temporary buildings, the local authorities strongly opposed the erection of this provisional hall on the acquired site. Undeterred, the congregation continued to erect their temporary wooden hall and completed it on Saturday, 9th March 1968. The initial services were conducted in the hall on the following day even though permission from the local council had not yet been granted.

During those early and formative years of the Hillsborough church the congregation was keen to find a pastor for the people. Their first attempt was to invite the Rev. Alan Cairns to be their minister, but he did not feel the Lord would have him leave Ballymoney where he was ministering. They then asked the Presbytery to place Rev. Gordon Cooke to work with them as a student minister. He diligently fulfilled that role from April 1967 until February 1968 when he left to become the minister of the Rasharkin church in County Antrim.

Rev. John Douglas, then minister of Moneyslane Free Presbyterian Church and interim moderator for the Hillsborough congregation, conducted another Gospel mission in the recently erected portable building. During those meetings another seventeen people were converted.

Following this mission Mr. Ian McVeigh was placed as a student minister under the supervision of Rev. John Douglas at the Hillsborough Church in March 1968. He remained there until November 1971 when he received a call to be minister of the Coleraine congregation.

The expanding church at Hillsborough soon outgrew the capacity of their portable hall, and it was obvious to the leadership that a larger and more permanent building would be necessary. At first, Revs. William Beattie and John Douglas looked at a property in Lisburn Street in the village. Again there was further opposition to the Free Presbyterians occupying this property in the heart of Hillsborough.

After some discussion the church agreed to purchase a site from Mr. James Anderson on the opposite side of the road from their temporary location in the portable hall. On 8th April 1972 the moderator of the Free Presbyterian Church, Dr. Ian Paisley, cut the first sod for the construction of a more permanent home for the church and returned three months later to lay foundation stones for the new building.

At that time Stanley and Ina Barnes with their daughter Heather could not have been aware that all of this preceding history at the Hillsborough Church was laying a good foundation for their future ministry. Immediately after Stanley took up his responsibilities as minister of the church in October 1972, he organised another two Gospel missions; one was with Ina's former minister, the Rev. S. B. Cooke, and the other was a youth mission which was conducted by the Rev. Ken Elliott from Portadown.

During those early months at his new charge Stanley was not only endeavouring to win the lost of Hillsborough for Christ and build up his congregation, uppermost in his mind was the construction of the new church building and helping to raise funds for the project.

Saturday, 22nd June 1974 was a big day at Hillsborough when Dr. Paisley declared the beautiful new church building opened to the glory of God, and the congregation entered into the new sanctuary. This was not only a giant step forward for Stanley and his flock, it also officially concluded a long and antagonistic saga the congregation had endured for their right to meet and worship in their own premises. For some time the local planning authorities had opposed and contested the construction of the new church.

The newly-constructed building had a capacity for 300 people, and when the congregation transferred from the packed portable hall to the new church they were glad to have a little more comfort and ample accommodation.

On his first Sunday morning in the new sanctuary Stanley chose Job

8:7 as his text: "Though thy beginning was small, yet thy latter end should greatly increase." This was a promise that the Lord had given him for that occasion. Even he was overwhelmed when that promise should be fulfilled much earlier than anyone could have anticipated.

The rapid growth of the congregation was undoubtedly partly due to Stanley's all-round pastoral work. His warm Bible ministry from the pulpit and his care and attention in the community proved to be very acceptable and profitable qualities.

Stanley's sermons were not long and most certainly were never boring. He has an exceptional ability to outline a biblical text or portion of Scripture, to make it simple to understand and enhance and enrich the content with suitable illustrations. Stanley's aptitude for reading widely and his retentive memory enabled him to quote at length from some of the great commentators and theologians. Furthermore, his reverence for the Scriptures and sincerity in his preaching did not mask his innate sense of humour. He always had a witty story to tell.

Stanley's ministry has always been greatly enhanced and enriched by Ina's discreet and effective role. She is of a quieter disposition than that of her husband, but just as faithful and efficient in discharging her responsibility as a dedicated pastor's wife. Solomon's appraisal of a virtuous woman in Proverbs 31:10 sits well with Ina: "her price is far above rubies." While Solomon's ancient estimation is still true of every good wife, it is particularly true of a valued pastor's wife. In many ways hers is the most difficult role. Although she was not called to be an assistant minister at the church, yet Ina played a vital part in the success of her husband's ministry. Besides caring for her own family and being a constant support at her husband's side, she was self-effacing in trying to serve the whole church family at Hillsborough. No member of the church was more loyal in attendance at the house of God than Ina. At the same time, she was a very kind and hospitable hostess at the manse. There was always a welcome at the door of the Barnes' home.

David Williamson described Ina very appropriately when he said, "Mrs. Barnes is a very quiet, but a very wise woman."

Ina needed to be a wise woman, for she had the formidable task of trying to keep her husband organised. Orderliness would not be a strong point with Stanley. Ina was a very able personal assistant, for she attended to all her husband's correspondence, typed up the weekly church announcements, prepared manuscripts, made his travel arrangements and at the same time, kept a check on his diary to make sure he turned up where he was scheduled to be. She was a true helpmeet.

Not long after their arrival in Hillsborough the Lord blessed Stanley and Ina with a son and a young brother for Heather. Andrew's birth was greeted with the same delight as when Heather was born. The happy parents felt their family was complete. It was with great gratitude that they dedicated their home to the Lord.

While the pastoral ministry in the Hillsborough church was an awesome responsibility, as Christian parents Stanley and Ina knew that their primary responsibility was to raise their two little children to fear the Lord and one day be able to lead them to personal saving faith in Jesus Christ.

The weekly congregation at Hillsborough was growing, and a large Sunday School also developed to educate the local children in the Holy Scriptures and Shorter Catechism. God blessed the church with a fine team of Sunday school teachers who dedicated themselves to this work. Stanley and Ina took a particular interest in the young people and often invited them to the manse for fellowship and supper.

It is not surprising that God called some of those young people into Christian work at home and abroad. Stanley's missionary experience helped him emphasise the need of depleted mission fields around the world. He frequently invited missionaries to his pulpit to share the burden they carried for their particular sphere of service. The inevitable response to these recurring challenges was that several members of the Hillsborough Church would step out in faith to serve God at home and abroad through various missionary agencies.

The promise that God gave to Stanley early in his Hillsborough ministry, "Though thy beginning was small, yet thy latter end should greatly increase," held true. Though the beginnings were not exactly small, a greater increase was yet to come.

Chapter 9

Sustained by Supporters

The growth of a church, like the growth of a soul, does not just happen. It requires total commitment on the part of the minister, sincere prayer, powerful preaching and hard work. The Apostle Paul's farewell address to the Ephesian church articulates the minister's role well:

> "Ye know, from the first day that I came... after what manner I have been with you at all seasons, serving the Lord with all humility of mind, and with many tears, and temptations, which befell me... and how I kept back nothing that was profitable unto you, but have shewed you, and have taught you publicly, and from house to house... neither count I my life dear unto myself, so that I might finish my course with joy, and the ministry, which I have received of the Lord Jesus, to testify the gospel of the grace of God... I take you to record this day, that I am pure from the blood of all men. For I have not shunned to declare unto you all the counsel of God...remember, that by the space of three years I ceased not to warn every one night and day with tears" (Acts 20:18-31).

The great apostle was not alone in his labours in the gospel. He was surrounded by true and loyal colleagues, or as Paul referred to them as his brothers in God's family, his companions in labour in the Lord's harvest field and fellow-soldiers in the good fight of faith.

At the Hillsborough church Stanley Barnes was also richly blessed to be surrounded and supported by a fine company of Christians in the fellowship of the local church. They were true companions-in-labour in serving the Lord of the harvest. They were also fellow-soldiers who were enlisted and committed to the Captain of their salvation in the ongoing spiritual battle against the powers of darkness. Without their support the work of the church could not have been accomplished.

The confines of this volume make it prohibitive to mention all those who made a vital contribution to the growth of the Hillsborough church. However, the role played by the Clerk of Session, David Williamson, cannot go unnoticed. David, a foundation member of the Hillsborough congregation, was a constant supporter of the minister, a true friend, a wise counsellor and a ready encourager for Stanley and Ina.

Although David was raised in a Christian home he was not converted until after he and Emilene were married. During the Christmas holidays of 1965 David discovered that Dr. Paisley was preaching at the Christian Workers' Union Hall in Lisburn on Boxing Day. Attending that meeting changed his whole life. Deeply convicted of his sin and guilt David suffered a sleepless night until he finally clambered out of his bed and, on his knees, called upon God for mercy and asked the Lord Jesus Christ to save him.

Until then David had been a member of a Presbyterian Church, but now as a Christian he was unhappy with the ecumenical trends of that church. At first he sought fellowship at Dunmurry Free Presbyterian Church where the Rev. William Beattie was the minister. While attending at Dunmurry David became involved in plans and preparation for the Rev. Beattie to conduct a tent mission in Hillsborough. These were the meetings that would ultimately result in the formation of the Hillsborough Free Presbyterian Church.

Throughout the weeks of the tent mission and right from the beginning of the Hillsborough church, David was fully committed to the worship, work and witness there. He was appointed to be the first superintendent of the Sunday School and was also elected to become a member of the church's original committee. In recognition of his continued devotion to the Hillsborough congregation, David was later ordained to be an elder and assumed the office as Clerk of Session. All of this development helped him build a very close friendship and working relationship with Stanley. In just about every way he has been the minister's right hand man. Like the biblical character, Barnabas, David Williamson was "a good man, and full of the Holy Ghost and of faith."

Although David's commitment and contribution is singled out here, he only epitomised a faithful body of elders, committee men, leaders of the ladies' and youth departments, Sunday School teachers, assistants in the crèche, talented musicians and a vast body of ready helpers.

The combined contribution of all these workers, plus Stanley's faithful ministry in the pulpit, his diligent pastoral care for the congregation and his leadership soon resulted in such a numerical growth in the congregation that the original church, which seated 300 people, soon became too small. On most Sundays the main sanctuary was not only filled to capacity, dozens of extra chairs also had to be put down the aisles and around the perimeter of the building to accommodate the increased number of people attending the services. The Sunday School also grew so much that the session and committee began to think of how they might increase the capacity of the premises to accommodate the growing number of children.

Under the pressure of this congregational growth, thoughts of building a new Sunday School complex were superseded by the suggestion of building a second church.

Work commenced on the new structure in March 1984. Mr. Shannon, whose farm was adjacent to the church property, graciously consented to sell an adjoining plot of land to the church at a very reasonable price. Although this neighbour was not a member of the Hillsborough church, yet when he was approached about the proposal, he answered,

"If this is for the extension of the Lord's Kingdom, who am I to stand in the way?"

The joyous celebration and thanksgiving planned for the opening of the new church building in September 1987 was overshadowed by the sudden death of one of the church's most dedicated workers, Jim Carlisle. Jim, a driver on the church buses, was working at the church site when he suffered a heart attack and died. His sudden home-call to heaven caused deep shock among the congregation. Subsequently, the church session decided to pay tribute to Jim by using the unfinished church building for the funeral Thanksgiving Service. During the ceremonies for the opening of the new building on the following Saturday a commemorative plaque was unveiled in memory of Jim Carlisle.

Dr. Paisley was present to declare the new and very impressive church building open to the glory of God on Saturday, 18th September 1987. The new structure cost a total of £500,000 and provided the church with a facility that was both beautiful and serviceable. Besides a suite of extra Sunday School rooms, an office and a well-equipped kitchen, the new church was built to comfortably seat 750 people - 600 worshippers on the ground floor and another 150 in the gallery. The former church building was adapted to be used for youth and fellowship meetings. These stunning new premises were surrounded with a very large car park, beautifully landscaped gardens and a substantial plot of ground designated as the church cemetery.

The new building added fresh impetus to Stanley's ministry in Hillsborough. It also added to the many ministerial pressures and duties of visiting the sick and needy, conducting funerals and, on happier occasions, officiating at weddings.

Besides accumulating one of the best Christian libraries amongst his Free Presbyterian peers, Stanley also embarked on writing books. His works cover devotional, biographical and historical themes. Many of these books highlight a subject that has been uppermost in Stanley's mind and ministry for many years - that of spiritual revival. Perhaps this is a reflection on the fact that his conversion occurred during the celebrations to mark the centenary of the great Ulster Revival of 1859. Stanley's passion for revival has still not abated after almost four decades of Christian ministry.

The success of the ministry at Hillsborough earned Stanley great respect among his ministerial colleagues, inside and outside the Free Presbyterian denomination at home and abroad. Their confidence in him and respect for his ministry was made abundantly clear when he was elected by his brethren to be Deputy Moderator of the Free Presbyterian Church of Ulster. He served alongside the Moderator, his friend, Dr. Ian Paisley, and was ever ready and willing to stand in for "the Doc" whose daily programme was always full. In his discharge of these weighty responsibilities Stanley was efficient, impartial and most effective.

The construction of the new church building at Hillsborough also reflected a more important emphasis which Stanley's fruitful ministry had brought about, the conversion of precious souls, the growth and maturity in faith of the church members and the church's influence beyond the boundaries of Hillsborough.

Right from its earliest days the Hillsborough church has been very missionary minded, and this was undoubtedly nurtured and advanced because of Stanley's own vision and commitment to missionary enterprise at home and abroad. Former members, Rev. Harry Cairns and Rev. Maurice Baxter, were called into the Christian ministry while members of the Hillsborough church. Several young men from the church went to study at the Whitefield College of the Bible near Banbridge. Norman and Angela McCready were commissioned by the church to serve God with New Tribes Mission in Papua New Guinea. Billy and Agnes Bryans served with The Faith Mission and

David Moore went from Hillsborough to study at Prairie Bible Institute in Canada and then into Christian ministry in that dominion.

It was with that same missionary interest and zeal that caused Stanley to seize the opportunity to be part of an arranged delegation to visit Romania early in February 1990.

During that trip to the recently liberated Eastern European country, Stanley requested for Tom Lewis to arrange a visit to what had formerly been an underground Baptist Church in Timisoara.

Tom was able to introduce Stanley to Eugen Groza who was the pastor at Bethany Baptist Church. It was Pastor Eugen who invited Stanley to share his testimony with the assembled congregation at the aforementioned Wednesday night church meeting.

That encounter with Pastor Eugen and his church took Stanley's missionary interest and zeal to a higher level and forged a bond between both men and their respective churches that would tell an unfolding story.

Stanley soon got to know more about Pastor Eugen.

Chapter 10

Missing on The Mountain

Eugen Groza was born in Transylvania, the central province at the heart of Romania's eight provinces. The Carpathian Mountains form a high arc-like ridge like the letter "U" across the whole region. The lower slopes and foothills of this mountain range are densely covered by the largest natural forests in the whole of Europe. The name Transylvania means "the land beyond the forests."

Nestled in the plains and valleys below these mountains are scores of small medieval villages made up of narrow streets of simple houses and fortified churches. The fertile countryside surrounding these small hamlets is composed of farmlands, cowsheds, sheepfolds and rural homesteads.

This same productive region has a long history of conflict and change. Up until World War I Transylvania had been associated with Hungary, but with the redrawing of European borders in 1918 the province became part of Romania. During the inter-war years the territory was hotly disputed between these two countries. Germany invaded Romania early in World War II. The head of state in Romania, King Carol, abdicated in September 1940, and the country passed into the control of the fascist and pro-Nazi Prime Minister, Ion Antonescu.

When the course of the war began to turn against Germany Ion Antonescu appealed to the Allies to save Romania from the horrors of the approaching Red Army and the threat of Soviet occupation.

At that stage, King Michael, son of the late and former King Carol, implemented a coup in which the pro-German Antonescu was arrested. The monarch then implored all Romanians and the remnant of the Romanian military forces, to fight with and not against, the invading Red Army. In 1944 King Michael finally signed an armistice with the Allies and declared war against an already-dying and retreating German army.

In August of that year nothing could stop the might of the Russian military advancing into Romania as they drove westwards for their ultimate defeat of the Nazis. By some of the population they were looked upon as the liberators of Romania, but in truth they enslaved the whole nation when they aided the Romanian communists to take over the entire country. These Marxist forces soon moved in to subdue any ethnic Hungarian resistance in Transylvania and annexed the whole jurisdiction under Romanian and communist rule.

King Michael was retained as a mere puppet monarch in Romania until he was finally forced to abdicate his position and leave the country in 1947.

In 1945, during the final stages of World War II, the future map of Europe was determined at the Yalta Conference convened between the American and British Allies and the Soviet Union. As a result of that conference, Europe was divided into two major spheres: the West under the influence of the Allies and the Eastern Bloc under the sway of the Soviet Union. With the redrawing of the European jurisdictions came the onset of the Cold War when Europe was divided East from West by the Iron Curtain. Consequently, Romania, like all the other Eastern Bloc countries, became a virtual satellite state of the Soviet Union.

It was widely acknowledged that throughout the period of Ceausescu's communist rule in Romania he had one of the most ruthless, pervasive and uncompromising governments of all the Soviet bloc countries. It is also recognised that this egoistic dictator rigidly followed the Soviet

Photographic Section

Pastor Proctor Emmanual Mission

John and Ellen Philips (Sunday School Superintendent).

Stanley at Judo class

Students at WEC, MTC

Be My Daddy

The scars of war

Mass rally in Bucharest

Soldiers side with the population

On the streets

Cemetery of Heroes - Memorial to those killed in the Revolution 16th -22nd December 1989

Be My Daddy

Eugene & Mihaela's Wedding

Bethany Baptist Church

Stanley and Eugen on Eugen's first visit to Northern Ireland

Be My Daddy

Boys from Recas in the orphanage

Supplies from N.Ireland

Unloading supplies

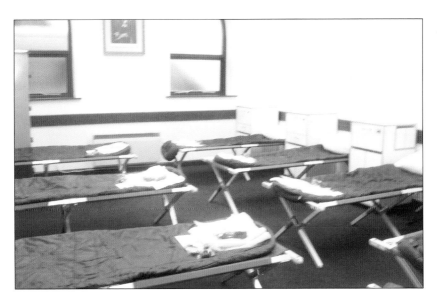

Church rooms were converted to dormitories

Be My Daddy

Boys from Recas

Onesimus boys at Stormont

Girls from Lugos Orphanage

Be My Daddy

Deborah girls en route to Northern Ireland 2012

Deborah girls outside their Hotel !!!

Photo Section

Deborah girls at Lyons Karting

Receiving gifts from the moderator Dr John Greer and his wife Joan

Visiting the harbour in Portavogie

pattern of imposing a burdensome repression on his own people.

Pastor Eugen Groza's parents, Petru and Apalina Groza, raised their six children in the Transylvanian village of Clopotiva. Despite the oppression of the communist government, they took their children to the little Baptist church in the village every Sunday. Mr. & Mrs. Groza were devout Christians and Petru was an elder in the local Baptist church.

Before Eugen was born, his mum and dad already had three children. The eldest of these was Eugenia, who later became a nurse. Petru is Eugen's eldest brother, and he later qualified as an engineer before going on to be the pastor of a Baptist church in Fagaras, Brasov County, Romania. Petru and Apalina Groza's second son was John.

Eugen, their fourth child, was born in October 1954. When he was only two years old tragedy hit the Groza family. His older brother, John, while he still was a young boy, went with his uncle to care for the family's sheep that were scattered on the mountain slopes. It was autumn, and on that day the grey mist rolled down from the towering mountains and enveloped the whole area in a cold and damp fog. After chasing sheep for some time on the mountain slopes John complained to his uncle that he felt cold and was hungry. The uncle still needed to attend to some other sheep so he told young John to go back down to the small house that was not further than 150 metres away on the side of the mountain and wait for him there.

As John withdrew he disappeared out of his uncle's sight to make his way back down the mountain. Sadly, young John Groza was never seen again. When the uncle arrived at the simple mountain house there was no sign of the boy. It seems that as he walked through the mist he never found the house. The despairing uncle searched frantically for his young nephew in the persisting mist and approaching twilight. Alas, he never found him.

It was with a heavy heart that the uncle returned to the village to raise the alarm and break the news of John's disappearance to his unsuspecting parents. Petru and Apalina Groza were beside themselves when they heard that John was missing. At the first light of the following day the whole village of Clopotiva turned out to search all over the mountain, in the gorges, the streams and the meadows, but they found no trace of young John. They never found any of John clothes, shoes or belongings. He had completely disappeared and was never found.

Mr. & Mrs. Groza did not give up their search for weeks afterwards, but they never found any vestige of their missing son. They were grief-stricken. Friends and neighbours tried to comfort them. Christians at the village Baptist church prayed for them and tried to care for them. Their ultimate comfort came from knowing that their missing son was with the Lord. They felt that like the Bible patriarch, Enoch, their son "was not, for God took him."

The only way that Petru and Apalina Groza could cope with their loss in the following years was to try to draw a line under the tragedy and devote their attention to loving and caring for the children they still had. In the years ahead they never spoke of the terrible incident to Eugen or the other children that were born into their family after young John's disappearance.

When Petru and Apalina's next son was born the distraught parents called him John. Perhaps this was their way of trying to fill the void their disappeared son had left in the home. This John would remain in Clopotiva through his adult years, and like his father, he became an elder in the local Baptist church. Maria was the final addition to the family, and like her older sister Eugenia, she also became a nurse. In time and in answer to their prayers, Mr. & Mrs. Groza had the immense satisfaction of seeing all the children profess faith in Jesus Christ while they were still children.

In those days school was not so important for most of the village people, but this was not the case with the Groza family. Mr. Petru Groza worked extremely hard in the forest all year round, in the heat of the summer and in the cold of the winter, to make enough money to be able to send all his children to study at the village school. Not many families in Clopotiva in those days shared Petru's firmly held views on hard work and serious study.

Eugen attended the village school through to eighth grade. Even as a young boy he enjoyed school and loved to study. At home Eugen with his two brothers and two sisters gladly listened to their mother tell their favourite Bible stories and they highly respected their father's faith. Even though Eugen liked church he was not always happy to go and sit through the long worship services every Sunday. The morning service began soon after breakfast at 9.00 a.m. and did not finish until noon; the evening service was another two-hour meeting. However, because he was only a young boy, Eugen felt he had no other option than to sit through these long services.

One day at school Eugen was glad to hear there was a possible alternative to going to church on Sunday mornings. The teacher announced that the local communist authority had organised for a movie to be shown for children at the village cultural hall every Sunday morning at 10.00 a.m., and the students were required to attend. A movie instead of church? It seemed to be a good idea for little Eugen and other children.

Eugen's parents were not too happy with this imposed arrangement, but because the school children were expected to attend they felt they had to conform. Besides the movie being cunningly arranged for the same hour as the church services, the communist authorities also used the movie-hour to try to indoctrinate the children. Before the main feature film they screened a fifteen-minute communist propaganda movie every Sunday.

Like some of his friends, Eugen tolerated the propaganda movie so that he could enjoy the main film, but the insidious ploy of the communists was to brainwash the children by constant repetition of their Marxist philosophy. Having accepted Eugen's absence from church on Sunday mornings for several weeks, Eugen's parents finally decided to withstand the pressure that was being imposed on their family. They made up their mind that from then onwards their children would be going to God's house instead of the cultural hall on the Lord's Day mornings.

Initially, Eugen was not too happy with his mum and dad's determination to withstand the school's Sunday arrangements, but in spite of his childish protests he knew he had to obey. When he returned to school on Monday the teacher asked all those who had not been at the cultural hall on Sunday morning to stand in the middle of a circle in the school playground. When the Groza children and several friends sheepishly stepped forward, all the other students were encouraged to laugh them to scorn. They chanted and called them fools because they went to church with old people and believed in God.

Embarrassed and humiliated by their friends, Eugen resolved within himself that when he reached high-school age he would leave home and not have to suffer this sort of persecution because his Christian parents believed in God and attended church.

There were very few luxuries for the residents of Clopotiva. The Grozas and their neighbours did not enjoy the benefit of electricity in their homes. The children had to complete their schoolwork at home by the light of oil lamps, and the evening services at the church also used similar lamps. Ironically, there was always a generator and sufficient diesel to show the movies on Sunday mornings.

All the Groza children had to help on their father's farm. Besides working with their parents in the fields they also had to tend to the livestock. This meant climbing the surrounding mountains and hills for the sheep and goats. With the tragedy that befell their other son

Petru and his wife were vigilant to look out for their other children.

The intense summer heat made the outdoor farming chores a little more acceptable. However, during the winter rains and storms the children were often soaked through and consequently they frequently suffered from colds and other bronchial illnesses. Later in his life these repeated illnesses would take a heavy toll on Eugen's health.

When Eugen was eight years old the country's socialist government imposed the collectivisation of Romanian agriculture. The aim of this collectivisation campaign was to usurp and incorporate all the privately-owned farms, their animals, farm implements and vehicles into one "great productive unit". The official propaganda at the time proclaimed this would be "the final victory of socialism in both the urban and rural areas." Soviet counsellors closely monitored this Marxist plan as the government officials went from one Transylvanian farm to another requisitioning the land and property. Farmers were obliged to sign official forms by which they consented to comply with the imposed programme.

While some of the farmers in Eugen's village readily complied with the new law, Petru Groza and some of his neighbours were opposed to the scheme and did everything to resist and evade the authorities. When they learned that the government officials were due in their area they fled to the mountains to try to avoid having to sign any forms. Sometimes the parents stayed overnight in the hills while their children remained at home. To counter this the socialist bureaucrats sometimes arrived at the farms unannounced or late at night in the hope of catching the farmers unawares.

After this game of cat and mouse went on for some time, the authorities started to demand from the children to tell them where their parents had gone. When they still failed to get any satisfaction from this ploy the heavy-handed officials resorted to threatening what might happen to the children if the parents continued to refuse to comply.

In spite of many protestations and attempts to avoid and evade the inevitable, Petru Groza and other neighbours had to finally give in and sign their farms over to the state authorities. Otherwise, they and their families would not have been able to survive.

Eugen always enjoyed his school lessons and was an avid reader. He also appreciated being part of the school's sports programmes. Romanians idolised their sporting heroes such as the volatile, but popular tennis star, Ilie Nastase, the outstanding gymnast, Nadia Comaneci and the brilliant soccer player, Gheorghe Hagi.

Eugen never aspired to these heights of sporting achievements, yet any hopes of a sporting career were dashed when he was only twelve years old. One morning he complained to his parents that his joints were very sore and he had pains in his ankles and feet. At first his dad discounted this as growing pains. Later that day it became evident that the pains were so bad that the poor lad could barely walk. His mum and dad realised that something serious was wrong with their son and took him to see the doctor.

After the doctor's examination Eugen was taken to hospital where he was diagnosed as having rheumatic fever. The medical consultant explained to Mr. Groza that Eugen was a very ill young boy and would have to undergo an intense course of antibiotics. Furthermore, the doctor explained that for the foreseeable future the boy would have to refrain from all physical sport. In addition to these restrictions placed on their young son, the Grozas became even more alarmed to learn that it was likely that Eugen was among the low percentage of juvenile patients who suffer long-term consequences from this fever; therefore, their son was kept under close observation because it was feared that rheumatic fever had affected the valves of his heart.

On his hospital bed Eugen began to mull over why this should be happening to him. He felt it was unfair that although he had been a good boy who attended church and learned the Bible verses, he should have to suffer. He could think of no good reason why God should be punishing him. He was a very troubled young man.

When Eugen recovered from his illness he returned to the village school. After he completed eight years at this grade school he left his family home to further his education at Technical High School in Cugir, a provincial town 100 kilometres from his village. The high school offered a five-year course, which was specifically designed to prepare students for a future in engineering.

For a long time Eugen had wanted to be free from the restraints of his Christian home and be able to lead, what he considered to be, "a more normal life." This new school had taken him so far from home that during the five years there his mother and father did not even visit him to see where he was living. Furthermore, as a teenager in Cugir he did not have to attend church.

Now that he had the freedom to do what he wanted Eugen began to indulge in things that had been prohibitive back home. He accompanied his new school friends to visit their homes, take part in youthful discos and enjoy their wild parties. Eugen tried to enter into all these self-indulgent pleasures to which they introduced him. However, try as Eugen did, all of these so-called, "new-found pleasures" did not give him the lasting satisfaction for which he longed.

His continued unhappiness and dissatisfaction resulted in Eugen feeling totally out of place. He often remained standing quietly in a dark corner while his friends seemed to be living it up. While he was disappointed with these worldly pleasures, at the same time he was not happy with God or any relationship with Him.

He thought to himself, *Maybe those Marxist and atheistic films have influenced me? I remember those Bible verses and my father's prayers, but I don't want to go back to church or religion.*

Eugen wondered where he would ever find real contentment and true satisfaction.

Chapter 11

Changes and Communists

While he was a student at Cugir Technical High School Eugen made excellent progress in his studies. During his fifth year the school principal announced that news had come through of a government bursary for the top three students to partake in a four-year engineering course in China. To live in Asia for four years sounded appealing to Eugen. He had always wanted to see the Himalayan Mountain range and visit the Great Wall of China. This would be an excellent opportunity to fulfil those dreams. At the same time, he did not want to run too far ahead of himself, so he diligently concentrated on his final exams and study so that he would qualify for this incentive.

Eugen could hardly believe what he was hearing when he learned that he had taken first place in his study group, and therefore, was offered the first of the three places for the course in China. He was so excited and relishing the great opportunity that he was already planning in his mind how he would prepare for the trip.

In his exhilaration he communicated his exciting news to his friends and his family back home. They shared in the delight of his success even though they were not too happy with the possibility of his going so far away from home and for so long.

Just when Eugen was getting used to the news of the trip to China a man arrived at the school several weeks later and made a point of speaking with Eugen. This man was an officer of the Securitate, the Romanian Secret Police. His pronouncement shocked Eugen. "You will not be able to go to China."

Eugen was stunned. His mouth fell open at the man's abrupt statement. After a minute's silence he asked the stranger, "And why not?"

"You are Baptist, and therefore, you cannot be trusted," the shady character answered.

"A Baptist? I am not a Baptist. My parents are Baptists, but I am not. I'm nothing," protested Eugen, ever so anxious to retain the hope of fulfilling his dream.

"You are a Baptist," the man insisted. "I know you are a Baptist, and that is the end of the matter."

Despite Eugen's objections, the stern man was not for relenting and walked out of the room. Eugen was devastated. His dreams were shattered. Again he began to reason within his own mind: *What is wrong with me? I have been away from home for four years and thought I had left all that religious stuff behind. Now it still follows me. Is God angry with me?* He was constantly haunted by all these soul-searching questions.

While Eugen wrestled with his disappointment, the mental turmoil and confused feelings he did not know that this was God answering the prayers of his concerned parents. They longed to see their son follow the Lord Jesus and even though he was a young man ready for university, they did not give up on praying for him.

With the China setback behind him and following his graduation from the Cugir Technical High School, Eugen made application to study for a Mechanical Engineering degree at the Technical University of

Timisoara. He was relieved to be offered a place.

During the Romanian hot summer of 1975 Eugen was glad to accept an invitation to go with a camp group from Timisoara up into the mountains for ten days where the atmosphere was less humid and the air a lot cooler. Two pastors accompanied the camping group as devotional speakers and spiritual counsellors. Besides revelling in the rustic living, mountain and forest hikes with all the fun and games, Eugen had some heart to heart talks with one of those pastors. It was then that he was able to unburden his heart and pour out all the pent-up feelings, frustrations and unanswered questions he had harboured for so long.

Before the ten-day camp had finished Eugen repented and got right with God. He not only poured his heart out to the pastor, he called upon God for mercy and surrendered his life to Jesus Christ. Even though it had taken longer than they had hoped, his parents' prayers were finally answered. Eugen came down from those mountains a different person. For the first time in his life he had peace and contentment in his heart - something that he had never known before.

Until then Eugen's life, outside of his studies, revolved around movies and sports. Now everything changed. His priorities were different. He wanted to read more of the Bible and join others for the fellowship and worship services at the church. On 10th August of that same summer he was baptised at a Baptist church in Timisoara. Eugen began to grow in his new-found faith by leaps and bounds.

Eugen soon discovered that it was not easy to be a Christian at university. Believers in every strata of society were under close scrutiny by the Securitate and were often harassed, deprived of promotions, denied privileges and sometimes detained for questioning. All this did not dissuade him from attending church. Every week Eugen joined a group of Christians from the First Baptist Church of Timisoara, Bethel Baptist, for a two-hour prayer and Bible-study meeting. Instead of always attending this same church at the weekend, he and another four or five companions often visited small churches in the many villages scattered over the countryside. They went to encourage these isolated believers and during those visits Eugen and his friends were often invited to sing, testify and preach.

Although this team of boys was making these frequent trips to encourage these isolated Christians, Eugen did not know that the Lord was also using these visits to prepare him for future service. Before he had ever thought of engaging in theological training Eugen was already learning how to preach the gospel. This unplanned training was invaluable and would help shape his ministry in future days.

While Eugen was studying in Timisoara in 1979 his eldest brother, Petru, met and married a girl from Fagaras and then set up home in the city. Eugen not only attended their wedding, but afterwards he paid periodic visits to their home during holidays. He took advantage of the opportunities to visit the local Baptist church in the city and through time he was even invited to preach at the church.

While he was on these occasional visits to Fagaras Eugen participated in the life of the Baptist church. At Christmas time he joined those who went carol singing or with the young people's day trips to the mountains to play in the snow. It was during these outings with the church that Eugen met a lovely young Christian woman from Fagaras whose name was Mihaela. It did not take long for Eugen to fall in love with Mihaela.

Even though he knew he had met the girl he wanted to marry, Eugen applied himself to his studies back in Timisoara. He enjoyed his academic course, and it seemed that his time at university flew by. When he graduated from the course with distinction in 1980, he and five other students were honoured by being invited to join the tutorial staff at the University of Timisoara. This was a very high honour indeed, but over the next few days Eugen came to the conclusion that it would be impossible for him to be a professor at the university and remain a Christian. He would therefore, have to decline the prestigious offer.

Eugen spoke with his professor about the dilemma he faced regarding the professorship. The learned and wise tutor advised Eugen not to make any rash decisions. It was required of all graduates who were selected to return and teach at the university that they spend two years working in an industrial plant. This was designed so that the tutor could gain experience in the work place before returning to the classroom. The professor advised Eugen to go and work in an engineering company for those two years and then see how things might develop when he finished.

That is exactly what Eugen did. Again this was providential. As an engineer Eugen had learned the importance of making things function with efficiency. He was not aware that God, who makes all things work together for good for His people, was quietly fashioning his whole future. Eugen moved from Timisoara to Hateg to engage in his first engineering job. Hateg is almost 150 kilometres from Fagaras, and although it involved a five-hour train journey, it really suited Eugen and his sweetheart, Mihaela. It meant they were able to visit each other more frequently.

It was a happy day on 15th November 1981 when Eugen and Mihaela exchanged their marriage vows at the Baptist church in Fagaras. At that moment their hearts swelled with gratitude to God how He had brought them together and now He was binding them together for life. Eugen had no doubts that Mihaela was the helper God had prepared for him. Over the next three decades she would stand with her husband to encourage him through the good times and very challenging times.

However, for six months after their wedding the newlyweds had to live apart. Eugen had to continue living in Hateg where he worked while Mihaela had to remain at her parents' home in Fagaras. This arrangement was forced upon them because his engineering job at the Hateg company was a government assignment, and he needed government approval before being able to move from one job to another. Furthermore, because Eugen was the only mechanical engineer in the Hateg company, the director there would not consent to him moving elsewhere. Consequently, the young couple had to be content with making short visits to each other as often as possible.

Not until the summer of 1982, seven months after they were married, were Eugen and Mihaela finally able to be re-united as husband and wife when Eugen finally got a transfer to another engineering company in Mihaela's home town of Fagaras.

After three years away from Timisoara and two years after Eugen and Mihaela had been married, he received a telephone call from his former professor at the University of Timisoara. The professor said that he had been speaking with the management of the company with which Eugen had been working and informed them that he would be approaching Eugen with an invitation to return to take up a lecturing position at the university.

This news seemed to come out of the blue for Eugen. He talked the proposal over with Mihaela and after considering the matter they wondered if the Lord was leading them back to the large city. It was impossible for people from the rural regions and provincial towns to gain employment in Timisoara or any large Romanian city without a licence issued by the city's authorities. However, the professor's invitation meant that Eugen and Mihaela would automatically be granted licences since he would be employed by the government.

Concluding that this move was God's will for them, Eugen consented to the offer of the tutorial position at the university. In the process of accepting the professorship he had to complete sixteen pages of questions about his personal life, his family, his wife and her family, his educational and professional background. To his surprise the paper made no reference about his views on religion or his belief in God.

In due course Eugen gained his licence and moved to Timisoara in September 1983. Until her licence to live in the city came through Mihaela had to remain with her family in Fagaras, which is almost 300 kilometres from Timisoara. Although the recently married couple had to suffer another six-month enforced separation, Eugen fitted into his teaching curriculum very well and was grateful to God for opening the door. Travel restrictions and these prolonged separations made life difficult for both of them, but early in 1984 Mihaela was finally able to join Eugen in Timisoara where they moved into a very small apartment in the city.

Just when it seemed that life for Eugen and Mihaela was evening out on a more level plain, Eugen was summoned to a meeting with the leader of the university's Communist Party. The man was quite aggressive as he asked Eugen why he had not become a member of the party. To this Eugen gave a glib answer and said that no one had ever invited him to join.

This was not the answer the belligerent man was expecting or wanting, and Eugen knew it. The communist leader became even more antagonistic and began to pour scorn on Eugen. "Why are you such a fool to believe in God nowadays when science is able to put men on the moon, and we have discovered so many other things that prove there is no God. If you continue to believe in God then there is no way you can work in this university. I want you to go away and write a paper in which you will admit that you do not believe in God any more and that you will not be attending church from now on. I will give you three days to hand me this paper."

Eugen felt amazingly calm and strong in spite of the gruff intimidation of the party leader. In replying he spoke up, "I don't need three days. I can tell you now that I will never write such a paper. I do believe in God and my Christian faith is very important in my life. Furthermore, you would not want to work with people who tell lies by writing one thing while they believe another. I am being honest with you. I believe in God and I will not tell lies or write falsehoods."

To this the angry communist said, "I will have to fire you. You cannot keep your job and still believe in God."

Eugen knew he could do one of two things. His employment and position at the university was legal; therefore, he could not be dismissed immediately. Moreover, the governors of the university would have to show good reason to sack him. On the other hand, he could have resigned on the spot and consequently, not have to enter into a whole process of contesting whatever decision the university authorities might reach. Eugen decided to take this latter route.

He went to consult another colleague and explained to him what had happened and his subsequent decision to resign from his position. He told his academic friend of his surprise that no question or reference had been made about his religion or faith in God when he filled in the questionnaire for the university position. To this the professor explained that there were unwritten laws within the university regime and these were firmly enforced. He said, "Eugen, you know that here in Romania there is freedom of religion and you can believe what you want. But you cannot be in education and be a Christian."

As a consequence of all this Eugen lost his position because his strong Christian views were untenable with those who hold educational posts and where they could influence others. Resigned to his new circumstances, Eugen also asked for this professor's help to secure another job in Timisoara seeing he still had a legal permit to work in the city. He was aware that the authorities might move to withdraw this licence at any time unless he had other employment.

After losing his tutorial role at the university in May 1984, just nine months after he had started, Eugen and Mihaela also lost the apartment that had been a fringe benefit with the university job. Thankfully, the professor kindly aided Eugen to find another job in engineering design soon after vacating his university position. With this job the couple were able to move into a very small apartment. Eugen was also able to gain employment for Mihaela in the same company.

Even while working in this new job the network of communist watchers and informers continued to dog Eugen's career. Because he was a Christian he was blatantly passed over for promotion. Even though those who were promoted to better positions were less qualified and less productive than Eugen.

The communist regime also created an atmosphere of fear and suspicion in the neighbourhood of their little apartment. The Securitate had their agents watching the Grozas. As a result of this, some neighbours ostracised them because they were Christians while others avoided them for fear of being seen in any sort of association with them.

It was not easy to be a Christian in Ceausescu's Romania.

Chapter 12

Who Will Prevail?

Eugen and Mihaela's home was wonderfully brightened and blessed when Adelina, their baby daughter was born in 1984. Little Adelina was the delight of their hearts, and her arrival certainly cemented the couple together after they had endured those long government imposed separations of the previous two years.

However, the happiness of their home was somewhat shattered on the following year when Eugen became seriously ill again. It seemed that the illnesses and physical weakness he had suffered as a young boy back home on his parents' farm had permanently damaged his health and left him with an enlarged heart. When his condition suddenly deteriorated at the end of 1986 the doctors concluded that Eugen was in cardiac distress and this was most likely a result of suffering from rheumatic fever as a child.

Initially, Eugen was hospitalised in Timisoara, but when it became clear that there was little that could be done for his condition medically in the city, it was decided in the spring of 1987 to transfer him to Targu-Mures, one of the only two hospitals in Romania where cardiac surgeries could be performed at that time. Targu-Mures was almost 350 miles away from Timisoara, and without any facility to accommodate families at the hospital it was prohibitive for Mihaela and her baby to be with Eugen. However, they and other members of his family tried to make periodic visits to him in Targu-Mures.

Although Eugen was a mature Christian he could not help being apprehensive about his future as he lay on the hospital bed. His thoughts were with Mihaela and their little girl, Adelina. He knew that his life was at risk. Many of the patients who had been around him when he arrived had died, some after surgery similar to that for which Eugen was waiting. He wondered what would happen to his wife and baby daughter if the Lord took him home to heaven. These troublesome thoughts prevented him from sleeping and often stole the peace from his heart. At the same time he committed his life to the Lord and asked God for His protection.

Thankfully, the Lord spared Eugen's life, and the surgery was successful. Nevertheless, the road to recovery was very slow. He spent two months in the Targu-Mures hospital before being allowed to return to his family in their Timisoara apartment. Mihaela was so glad to have her husband back home again, and Eugen was ever so glad to see how baby Adelina was growing to be a beautiful young girl.

This prolonged period of unemployment due to ill health resulted in Eugen forfeiting his job. At the same time he had been able to make the most of his convalescent months to read and study the Bible. He indulged in reading Bible commentaries and other theological books that were smuggled in to him.

It was hard for Eugen to understand why he had to go through those months of illness, surgery, convalescence and unemployment. Unknown to him at that time, the Lord was gradually working out His plan to equip Eugen for a new door that opened soon for him.

After his conversion in the summer of 1975 and at the start of his university course in Timisoara, Eugen began to attend Bethel Baptist Church in the city. It was with this church that he engaged in visiting outlying villages on various weekends during the months that followed his conversion.

In 1979 there were five Baptist churches in Timisoara. One was a German-speaking church; another was for those who spoke Hungarian, and the other three were Romanian. In November of that year a group of Baptist believers from Bethel Baptist decided to try to open a new church work in the Dâmbovita/Freidorf district of the city. Eugen knew the pioneers of this work, for he had attended prayer meetings with these people in various homes where they had been asking God for some time for guidance for this new church plant.

The new group enjoyed the approval and support of the leadership at the First Baptist Church in Timisoara and other local churches also. At first it was not easy to find a meeting place because of the communist restrictions imposed on all churches. However, through the generosity and sacrifice of the Toader family the new group was able to open a meeting place adjacent to his residence in Comuna din de Paris street.

Right from the beginning Eugen sensed the Christian love for the Saviour and rich fellowship amongst these believers that characterised this committed group of Christians. Even though it was his final year as a student in Timisoara he identified with the new church group which was named Bethany Baptist Church. It was so named to reflect the love, hospitality, devotion and worship our Lord experienced in the Bethany home of Mary, Martha and Lazarus. The Timisoara group wanted the Saviour to be as much at home amongst them as He obviously had been in Bethany, near Jerusalem.

Although Eugen had been absent from Timisoara for almost four years he never forgot his friends at Bethany Baptist Church, and when he returned to the city to teach at the university he was glad to renew fellowship with them. When the church was originally formed on 18th September 1979, seventy-three believers registered as members of the congregation. By the time Eugen arrived back in town in 1983 the congregation had almost doubled. Within a short time the Bethany

Baptist Church grew to become the largest underground church in all Romania.

This growth was in spite of the communists trying to steamroll the Christian church into silence. After the Romanian communists seized power with the invasion of Russia's Red Army in 1944, they ruled the country with an iron fist for the next forty-five years. Besides embarking on a campaign to eliminate all other ideologies, the atheistic communists declared war on all religion - especially Christianity. The predominant religion of the land was the Christian Orthodox Church followed by other smaller groups within Christendom, including many evangelical groups.

During the first twenty years of communist rule the Romanian government embarked on a series of Stalin-like policies in a brutal attempt to purge their society of all religion. During these two decades hundreds of professors, teachers, priests and pastors were executed, and hundreds more, like Pastor Richard Wurmbrand, were imprisoned, kept in solitary confinement and tortured for many years.

Pastor Wurmbrand reported of those days:

> Now the worst times came; the times of brainwashing. Those who have not passed through brainwashing can't understand what torture it is. From five in the morning until ten in the evening... seventeen hours a day... we had to sit just like this [he sat straight looking forward]. We were not allowed to lean. For nothing in the world could we rest a little bit-our head. To close your eyes was a crime! From five in the morning until ten in the evening we had to sit like this and hear: 'Communism is good. Communism is good. Communism is good. Communism is good. Communism is good. Christianity is stupid! Christianity is stupid! Christianity is stupid! Nobody more believes in Christ. Nobody more believes in Christ. Give up! Give up! Give up!' For days, weeks, years, we had to listen to these things!

After Nicolae Ceausescu came to power in 1964 he initially tried to exploit the Cold War stand-off between Eastern and Western bloc countries by courting the favour of United States and United Kingdom. He refused to take part in what was known as "the Prague Spring" when Russian tanks invaded Czechoslovakia in 1968 to quell an upsurge of protest against communist rule. Although Romania was a member of the Warsaw Pact countries Ceausescu gave the illusion of him being an anti-Soviet maverick by signing up to some international accords, including the Helsinki Agreement of 1975. By pledging his nation to abide by the Helsinki Agreement, Ceausescu, among other things, was agreeing to:

> Refrain from the threat or use of force
> Respect for human rights and fundamental freedoms, including the freedom of thought, conscience, religion or belief
> Equal rights and self-determination of peoples
> Fulfilment in good faith of these obligations under international law

As a result of consenting to these international values Ceausescu was hailed as a friend of the West and was enthusiastically welcomed on a Head of State visit to China where the Red government put on one of the most spectacular shows for any foreign visitor. President Richard Nixon and President Jimmy Carter received President Ceausescu with great honour in Washington. During these visits the Ceausescus were showered with expensive gifts of furs, diamonds and even a Lincoln Continental vehicle. Not to be outdone by the Americans, in 1978 President Ceausescu and his wife were even hosted by the Queen at Buckingham Palace.

While Ceausescu was enjoying VIP treatment abroad Christians in Romania could not believe what was happening. For them it was incredulous that this despot was being taken by the hand in the West and treated to these grandiose state visits around the world. However, the Ceausescu regime could not hide the massive discrepancy of what was really happening back in Romania. His government continued to enforce its oppressive policies on those who did not comply with his dictatorial rule even though the tyranny was not so explicit as it had been in previous years. To help his image abroad Ceausescu's methods to continue subjugating the Romanian people might have become more subtle, but they were not less aggressive, and he was still forcefully anti-God.

Under Ceausescu's directives the secret police employed more than 11,000 agents and had registered a half-million informers. The Romanian Securitate was one of the most brutal secret police forces in the world, responsible for the arrests, torture and death of thousands of people. However, they went about their sinister work in a less blatant way.

Christian leaders were under constant surveillance and were repeatedly interrogated, and some were sent to prison. Many dissenting pastors disappeared or were killed in what was reported as "traffic accidents". Families were left to mourn in silence for their missing loved ones. Others were charged with made-up charges of offences against the state and subsequently sentenced to long prison terms with hard labour. These prisoners were sent to all parts of the country and some were even forced to work on Ceausescu's grotesque palace in Bucharest. Dozens of these poor victims died of exhaustion and disease.

The Securitate carefully monitored religious communities because they were perceived to be potentially destabilising and obstructionist forces against Romania's socialist society. For that reason Securitate officers frequently forced their way into homes and church offices. Microphones were planted to record incriminating conversations. Telephone conversations were routinely monitored, and all internal and international fax and telex communications were intercepted. Threats were made against church leaders and their children. Sons and daughters of believers and Christian leaders were systematically harassed at their schools. Informers infiltrated seminaries. Church denominations were restricted when trying to open new church buildings, and theological colleges were allowed to graduate only two pastors each year.

On four different occasions Eugen Groza was called in for questioning about his church activities, and on one occasion he was almost caught by the Securitate when he was accompanied by an English preacher at an illegal Bible teaching class. As the secret police called at the front door of the house Eugen and his English friend were escaping out the back door. It was a close shave for both men.

Paradoxically, after forty-five years of communist rule and constant persecution, church membership had greatly increased and individual believers were stronger than they had ever been before. This bears out the promise Jesus Christ made in Matthew 16:18: "I will build my church; and the gates of hell shall not prevail against it." This promise admits that the infernal powers of darkness will militate against His church, but it also assures us that Jesus Christ, the great Head of the church, always prevails.

Forty-five years of atheistic communism destroyed many of the normal human values in Romanian society. In a free society, every man is born with a sense of responsibility to their family, their children and for himself. When a person is born and raised in a communist society where the individual owns nothing and the State owns everything, the size and location of their house is determined by the State, their job is allocated by the State, their children are educated by the State and all travel is limited by the State. As a result, all sense of personal responsibility is eroded.

Generally speaking, during the communist years in Romania all incentives to succeed in a career evaporated because the highest places were not awarded on merit. They were reserved for party members. People were not encouraged to use their initiative as they were prohibited from attempting anything new unless it was under the government's directive and supervision. A sense of personal responsibility and community trust also disappeared because people were fearful to speak of politics or complain against the State. Above all else, by trying to eliminate God from society, the communists created a perilous vacuum where morals collapsed and the morale of the people was brought very low.

In spite of the antagonism of the local authorities and the subtle ploys of the Securitate agents, the faithful members of Bethany Baptist Church pressed on with their determination to open their first church building. A Christian friend gave them a house, which they converted into a meeting place. This make-shift sanctuary was to be the home of their "illegal" underground church for the next eleven years.

Chapter 13

Turmoil in Timisoara

Eugen's enforced convalescence following his illness in 1987 not only gave him time to read and study the Bible, it also deepened his desire to know God more and to be able to serve Him. There were very few good theological books available in the Romanian language. During his years in education Eugen had become proficient in reading and speaking English. This would be a great blessing to him for his entire future ministry, but it was especially useful at this time when he was able to borrow and buy some English evangelical books. If the book was borrowed, Eugen took the time and painstaking effort to copy the contents of the book by hand writing page after page.

As Eugen's health improved he and Mihaela were able to return to the church family at Bethany Baptist Church. At the same time, he enrolled in a clandestine theological seminary, which was being offered to would-be servants of God. Ceausescu's oppressive communist regime restricted Bible and pastoral training in all churches in the hope of spiritually starving and suffocating the church from training potential future Christian leaders. Christian colleges were virtually non-existent and seminary education, although allowed, was closely monitored by the government. This was due in part to Ceausescu's desire to indoctrinate young and old in an atheistic mentality. He went so far as to imprison priests, pastors, and church leaders. In the realm of education Communist authorities restricted the number of students who could attend seminary.

In 1979 the missionaries of Navigators who specialised in Christian Bible-teaching and memorisation programmes secretly entered into Romania. They had hoped to introduce their excellent courses and programmes to the Romanian churches and thereby equip and prepare Christian workers. Sadly they did not stay for very long.

About the time the Navigators missionaries left Romania another underground organisation arrived in Romania: BEE International (Biblical and Theological Education by Extension). As the name of the mission suggests, this work was designed to send Christian missionaries and Bible teachers from the West, sometimes at great personal risk, to make periodic and covert visits to various locations to teach Bible and theology to small study groups. Students were officially matriculated for the properly structured course, and it was expected that those who enrolled would be committed to complete the study programme. Theological seminaries in the West validated the courses and offered diplomas and degrees for the students.

Tom Lewis, for many years a missionary with European Christian Mission (ECM) and present Director of BEE International in United Kingdom, was one of these missionaries. Through a network of contacts he had built up in Romania over many years, Tom was introduced to Eugen and other students in the Timisoara area. Tom was glad to enrol these men in the clandestine BEE theological training programme. For ten years before the revolution Tom and his friends had made frequent visits to Romania and on these trips they had smuggled Bibles and suitable Christian theological books to the BEE students. Over this period he struck up an enduring friendship with Eugen Groza.

Eugen was introduced to the BEE programme in 1980 and continued to be an avid student under the guidance of BEE International tutors until the Revolution occurred at the end of 1989. His training years were interrupted because of his employment in distant Hateg and the prolonged period of his illness. Nevertheless, he gleaned the maximum from the rich Bible courses and was able to earn a Master's degree with his specialty in Old Testament studies.

Although Eugen had already been a keen academic for several years, he enjoyed studying the scriptures in depth and made the most of those studies by leading the small congregation in further Bible lessons. This exercise created in Eugen a passion to read and study the Bible more and then impart what he had gleaned to the members at Bethany Baptist Church.

Over a period of time Eugen's maturity and ministry helped him progress and emerge into a place of leadership in the congregation. God blessed him and Mihaela even though he was an illegal student who was leading an illegal church. It is not surprising that the Bethany congregation continued to grow.

It was during Eugen's development into his leadership role that the sudden turmoil and chaos of the Revolution was unexpectedly thrust on Timisoara. Eugen tells of that time in his own words:

> Through all these days of oppression we wondered what was going to happen to Romania and what the future might hold for our children. Because the burden on our hearts was so heavy, we had seasons of prayer and fasting to ask God to intervene. We wanted and needed to see God break through. He was our only hope.
>
> In 1989 we became aware that Mikhail Gorbachev's "Perestroika" was bringing a lot of change to Eastern Europe. The Solidarity movement in Poland ushered in a national revolution. The popular Civic Forum threw off the shackles of communism and changed Czechoslovakia. Support for the Democratic Forum in Romania's neighbouring country, Hungary, saw the demise of bankrupted communist rule. In East Germany the people danced on the streets of Berlin all though the night when the unpopular

East German regime collapsed and the Berlin Wall began to be pulled down.

While all this was happening elsewhere, Ceausescu ordered Romania's borders to be sealed in an attempt to stem the tide of revolution and retain the pure communist ideology. He still believed in what he called "The Golden Dream" and even boasted that communism was stronger in Romania than it was in Russia or any other Eastern bloc country.

That all changed on 15th December 1989. While the other revolutions in these Soviet dominated countries were mostly bloodless transitions, that was not to be the case with Romania. A great price had to be paid by the people for their Romanian liberty.

It all started in the city of Timisoara where we lived, and I was part of the events leading up to Romania's Revolution. I saw many terrible things during those days. Looking back it is hard to describe it all and still more difficult to understand the forces that were behind it. Even today, I could give a lot of details of what I saw with my own eyes, but very little is written about this. I know there are many people who were guilty of terrible atrocities and they are still alive today. We will never find out the truth about all that happened during those December days of Romania's Revolution in 1989.

As I said, it really started on 15th December 1989 with the Hungarian Reformed Pastor, Laszlo Tökes. He had been giving interviews to articulate the people's protests against the land reforms that were being introduced by the communist authorities. In order to usurp more agricultural land the authorities insisted in moving people away from their villages and farms to be housed in monstrous apartment blocks in the cities. The real reason behind this was that they judged that people were easier to control when they lived in these high-rise apartments than on the scattered farms. People were very much attached to their land, but Ceausescu wanted to control them.

In his opposition to this Pastor Tökes was giving some interviews to a Hungarian radio station on that day. When his activities became known to the secret police they were concerned of the effect his words might have on Timisoara, a university city. To avoid the possibility of an uprising among students the Securitate decided to move Pastor Tökes to the northern part of the country, far away from any potential student support.

Accordingly, the authorities determined the deadline day in which the pastor would be evicted from his home and moved to a rural region. However, Pastor Tökes, knowing beforehand that they had planned the eviction for Friday, 15th December, told his congregation what was being planned, and therefore, he invited them to come to the parsonage to surround the church house on that day.

As he had requested, members of Pastor Tökes' congregation gathered outside his house on Friday afternoon to sing Psalms and read prayers. When the police arrived they went inside the house to remove the pastor and his family. News of the Securitate arrival spread quickly and within a short time the crowd outside swelled to several hundred people. They blocked the thoroughfare to prevent the removal of the pastor and his family. In an attempt to quell the agitation and threatening mayhem the Mayor of Timisoara, Petre Mot, was called. He appealed to the crowd to go home and tried to guarantee that nothing would happen to the pastor. The people refused to believe the mayor and declined to abandon their vigil.

News of what was happening spread quickly around Timisoara and within a few hours the crowd had swollen to several thousand people. At this the authorities sent in the riot police to disperse the growing mass of people. At first they employed their usual bully tactics to which they had been accustomed. However, on this occasion the people turned on them and the riot police had to flee for fear of the angry multitude, which was growing constantly. The police returned armed with water cannons to scatter the people. After a few skirmishes the crowd seized the cannons, broke them up, and threw the parts into the river. By this time roving riots ensued all over the centre of the city.

While this was happening Ceausescu was on an overseas visit to Iraq. In his absence, two military generals were dispatched from Bucharest on that Friday night to take charge of the worsening situation in Timisoara. It was around midnight that the first violence began when the generals sent the riot police back on to the streets with tear gas. This action scattered the multitudes through the back streets and to the outlying areas of the city. As they went the people were calling other citizens to join them in the protest and street demonstration. By this time the crowds had increased to tens of thousands and were active all over the city.

It was at that late hour that the first shouts of "Down with Ceausescu" were heard in the city. "Down with the regime!" and "Down with Communism!"

Cars were set alight on the streets and the back streets to try to impede the advances of Securitate officers and armed militia. All through the night the people were singing, chanting and many of us were earnestly praying for God's intervention.

In the middle of all this mayhem, Pastor Tökes and his wife were arrested by the Securitate and held prisoner in a farmhouse in the countryside.

These truly were momentous days for Romania and perilous times for the people.

Chapter 14

Revolution is in the Air

Eugen Groza can still hardly believe how God answered their prayers when he recalls the events of mid-December 1989. His city, Timisoara, was thrown into chaos and torn between the popular support of the masses for change and the oppressive and heavy-handed measures of Nicolae Ceausescu and his communist government.

Eugen continues his story:

> At the break of day on Saturday morning the streets cleared, but throughout the day there was a sense of crisis and pressure all over the city. The demonstrations and protests mostly took place through the night.

> That Saturday evening a strange thing happened. The large windows of the shops and commercial offices all over the centre of the city were broken. The government had sent in teams of men with long sticks to break these windows. When this happened some people did try to loot the shops. These looters had fallen for the government's ploy of trying to blame the popular uprising on the rioting and looting. The truth is that there was not very much for the looters to steal, for most of the shops were bereft of any stock. It was clear that the whole episode was orchestrated by the government to give them an excuse to justify their heavy-handed tactics and attack the crowds. Subsequently, 900 people were seized on the streets by the Securitate and taken into custody.

On Sunday morning I wakened very early and could not get over to sleep again. I decided to go down town and walk through the city centre. I did not know that this was to be the worst day of the Revolution in Timisoara. When I was in the city centre at seven o'clock that morning I could physically feel a great weight on my heart. It was a strange sensation - something I had never felt before or since. The heaviness in the air was so great that I began to touch all over my body to make sure there was nothing wrong with me. I looked up into the air to see if there was any reason for this heavy feeling. I just did not know what was going on.

Now that I can look back on it all I can only account for that eerie atmosphere as evil spirits being present over the city. The powers of darkness were about to be thrust on the people and the city plunged into a terrible blood bath.

As on the two previous days the people of Timisoara gathered in the city centre. It was then that the special troops, under Ceausescu's orders, began to randomly shoot with machine guns and live gunfire on the people. Scores of people, including women and children, were mowed down on the streets and in the parks and cemeteries.

Two young girls from Bethany Baptist Church, their father was an elder in the church, were shot outside the cathedral in the city centre. They were taken by ambulance to the hospital. Many people believe they were really killed in the hospital. Their parents never found the bodies of their daughters. This was not an isolated case. The same thing happened with many other families. Later we discovered that the corpses of those girls and dozens of other victims were taken in refrigerated trucks to Bucharest. There the unidentified corpses were cremated and their ashes callously but cunningly thrown into the river so that no proof could be brought against the perpetrators of these crimes.

One of the most despicable events of that black Sunday happened at the front of the cathedral when an ambulance arrived. The people flocked near to the emergency medical vehicle as many were injured and others were dying. To their horror, when the ambulance doors opened they were confronted with another troop of armed soldiers who opened up with machine guns on the unsuspecting crowd. People scattered in every direction. Some fled for refuge in the cathedral only to find that the doors were locked. Afterwards there was a bitter debate about who locked the doors of the church and thus prevented the people from finding protection.

After the first onslaught of random shootings army tanks and heavy military machines ploughed through the city chasing the thousands of people in every direction. The carnage continued until after dark but even with this the people did not surrender to the government's military might. I remember that in the early hours of Monday morning it began to rain. With this people sought shelter in doorways and any place they could, but most of them refused to go home. The majority of us did not sleep for three days and three nights through all this mayhem.

Early next morning I remember walking through the streets and seeing blood stained clothing scattered over the roadway and pavement and broken glass everywhere. On that day, Monday, many companies went on strike, and on Tuesday nearly all industry in the city was shut down. Thousands of workers marched from these industrial sites to the centre of Timisoara, singing patriotic songs as they went. Many of these traditional and national songs had been banned since 1947. By the time the industrial demonstrators got to the city centre the crowds had swollen to over 150,000 people.

We all sensed that this was the end of communism in Romania. There was no turning back from this. However, we learned later that at that time Ceausescu gave orders to bomb the whole city of Timisoara to stop the Revolution. As I already said, we did not go home or sleep for three days and three nights. We stayed in the centre of the city to protect the emerging leaders of the Revolution. We joined hundreds who knelt down on the streets and prayed, often repeating the Lord's Prayer so that others could join in. We sang many Christian songs and chanted loudly, "God exists! God exists! God exists! God exists!" Those were very moving scenes.

Throughout that week the army surrounded Timisoara in an attempt to contain the Revolution to our city. No one was allowed to leave the city and all telephone connections to the city were cut off. That meant that no news that might influence the rest of Romania could be sent in or out of Timisoara.

On Wednesday, 20th December, Ceausescu arrived back in Romania. Soon after his arrival he gave an interview on national television. He said that he had declared a state of emergency in Timisoara. Until that hour the dictator never admitted there were any problems in Romania. On his travels he tried to portray his country as a utopia of tranquility where everything was ideal and functioned well. The situation that had developed in Timisoara brought a reality check on what Ceausescu had been saying.

The president went on to announce that he was calling the people to a mass rally to support his regime in front of the Central Committee Building in Bucharest on the following day. Over the years these stage-managed public rallies had been commonplace in the nation's Capital.

On Thursday, 21st December, thousands of workers were bussed from their workplaces with banners and placards to hear Ceausescu speak. It was reckoned that up to half a million people came on to the streets of the capital for that rally.

At first, Ceausescu began his speech with a rant in which he blamed the unrest in Timisoara on the influence of the CIA and KGB and vowed that Romania would not fall. However, instead of applauding him as had usually happened in former rallies, shortly after he began to speak, shouts of "Timisoara, Timisoara" were heard from various sections of the crowd.

The volume of protest became louder and louder and was soon accompanied with jeers, boos and whistles. Ceausescu hesitated in his flow of speech and then tried to continue for a while. He could not speak over the tumult of the jeers or ignore seeing many pro-government banners being ripped up. He slowly brought his ill-fated speech to a close.

The dictator was clearly angered and for some moments there was a commotion among those on the balcony while Ceausescu was still being filmed for national television. Everyone could see that he was badly shaken and in that moment he appeared to be weak and vulnerable. He returned to the microphone to address the crowds with offers of wage increases for the workers. It was obvious to all that he was in desperation to retain his power over them. However, the masses had heard his rhetoric too many times. Now, they were not in the mood to be appeased by Ceausescu's hollow promises.

Very soon the crowds in the city began to grow as more and more people left their homes to head into the streets. They burned posters and photographs of Ceausescu and chanted "Timisoara! Timisoara! Timisoara!"

The secret police began to fire tear gas into the crowds, but wave after wave of people just kept coming into the streets, ignoring the presence of tanks. Police, the Securitate and the Army began to open fire with live ammunition on the crowds. Sporadic shooting continued throughout the night. On the next morning the people returned into the streets in even greater numbers

Street fighting continued to be very heavy in Bucharest with a major firefight for the control of the government. Raging battles focused on the state television and radio stations. A major confrontation ensued at the Bucharest airport between the military and Ceausescu's elite Securitate forces.

It was learned later that during those first days of the street protests when tens of thousands of Romanians marched through Bucharest, Ceausescu told the army to open fire on the demonstrators. It is commonly known that he had given this barbarous order to the National Minister of Defence, General Vasile Milea. When the general refused to obey he was charged with treason.

On the morning of 22nd December, in an inner chamber of the Central Committee's Palace, General Milea suffered a single shot wound to the chest. This was supposed to have taken place when he was seated at a table while speaking on the phone to his wife, Nicoleta. She said that after a few short words the line went silent for a while. After that she heard the noise of a struggle and then a single gunshot. A few moments later an officer lifted the phone and spoke to the General's wife to inform her that her husband had taken his own life. The General's family maintains that he was callously shot by Ceausescu's henchmen.

When it became obvious that there was no way back to communist and Ceausescu rule, large swathes of the Romanian Army began to defect to the side of the protesters.

A disillusioned Ceausescu emerged once more on the balcony of the Central Committee building with a loud hailer to appeal to the masses. He immediately became the focus of rage as the crowd tried to storm the building. Ceausescu, his wife, and their entourage just managed to escape in an overloaded helicopter from the roof of the Central Committee building.

They fled to a military camp near to the city of Târgovite, about 100 kilometres north of Bucharest, and thought they would have refuge there. However, two days later he and his wife were detained at the camp.

After a short trial on Christmas Day 1989, Nicolae Ceausescu and his wife, Elena, were executed.

Eugen and all Romanians knew that Romania was changing.

He also knew that God was answering prayer.

Chapter 15

Learning to Live with Liberty

Change came to Romania rapidly and dramatically. After forty-seven years of communist rule they had suddenly found freedom. This new liberty had been gained at an enormous price, and those who gave their lives for it should never be forgotten. At the same time, it should not be ignored that there were many concurrent and favourable situations and conditions which greatly aided and stimulated the Revolution. Most of these could not have been humanly engineered or manipulated. Eugen concludes that these propitious concurrences were undoubtedly in the providence of God.

Eugen relates his thoughts on this as follows:

> This was the beginning of change in Romania, and I often wonder why God used a pastor to initiate the Revolution. When the Securitate targeted Pastor Laszlo Tökes they could not have known what the outcome of their actions would lead to. The fact that they pursued a man of God suggests that God's hand was behind this event. It is not the usual role for a pastor to become embroiled in political and civic matters. I think the pastor's principal work is to promote spiritual revival while it is the general role of politicians to bring about political change. But in Romania God used a pastor to initiate political and social revolution.
>
> I believe that God did this to honour the stand of Christian believers, for they were the only people in Romania who did not bow their heads to communism. During Ceausescu's rule over us we recognised that the

highest authority in our land and in the world is God and not communism or Ceausescu. This confidence in God gave us strength to be able to stand against the constant oppression and opposition during those difficult years.

Amazingly, even though it was winter and December when normally it is very cold in Romania and the temperature is -10C, the Lord gave us a period of very mild weather during that crucial week. December 1989 was the warmest December for over a century. Even during those nights when the people were on the streets the temperature did not drop below 10C. This could have come about only by God's design. For us it was nothing short of a miracle.

Furthermore, when Ceausescu called the people together for a mass rally in the centre of Bucharest on 21st December, he facilitated the demonstrations against him and his regime. Romanian society was permeated with suspicion and fear of neighbours and even at times of their families. No one knew who the informers were. Therefore, it would have been impossible for some outside body or organisation to arrange a mass demonstration against the government. For individuals to try to do so would have put their lives in danger. However, the head of state, Ceausescu himself, called for the mass public gathering. In truth, just like the story of Haman in the Bible's book of Esther, he prepared the gallows on which he himself was hanged. He could never have imagined that he would not only lose power so quickly, but that he and his wife would also lose their lives so unceremoniously.

I have no doubt that God was behind all these factors. We had been asking God for deliverance, and this was His answer. That being the case, it also gives us great confidence for the future of Romania. Practically speaking, I do not have any great optimism for the future of our country, but I believe that when the Lord starts something, He will not leave it half done. He will complete it.

Many people gave their lives to bring political freedom to our country. I believe that Christians must be prepared to give their lives to bring spiritual liberty to our country. Jesus Christ is the only hope for Romania. I perceived that the Revolution left many people in a vacuum for which they were not prepared. They got rid of Ceausescu and communism, but they were left with an emptiness in their hearts and lives which only Jesus Christ can fill.

I also sensed that the Revolution in Romania presented the Romanian church with an excellent opportunity to present the Gospel to our own people. It is this conviction which motivated us at our church, Bethany Baptist Church, to not only reach out to the general populace but also to come to the aid of the countless numbers of orphans, to reach the pitiful young delinquents on our streets, to rescue the many abused girls and give hope to hundreds of prisoners who are crammed into our jails.

Before the Revolution churches were forced to remain inside their own walls. It was forbidden for us to engage in any social work. With the new opportunities freedom has brought, we are trying to make up for the time and generations we lost. Because of that, we got involved in several orphanages in various towns.

Immediately after the Revolution the leadership at the Bethany Baptist Church invited me to become their full-time pastor. Until then and during the days prior to the Revolution, I had been fully involved in the work there, preaching at the services and leading the weekly Bible studies for the congregation.

Corresponding with this invitation from the church I also received a request from the university in Timisoara from which I had been dismissed to return to my former position as professor of mechanical engineering.

At first, I felt torn between these two possibilities. I loved being an engineer. That is what I had trained for. On the other hand, I was reminded that on several occasions in my life I had been near to death, and the Lord had protected and preserved me. At various times I had been interrogated by the secret police because of my illegal work in the underground church. I might have been sent to prison as had happened to many other pastors. I believe the Lord safeguarded me from this also.

When I considered how God had preserved and protected me through all these illnesses and dangers I could only conclude that He had a purpose for my life. That helped me make the decision to accept the invitation to become the pastor at Bethany Baptist Church.

Now, with the benefit of hindsight, I am very pleased that the Lord enabled me to make that decision. I am just amazed how much God has blessed our work and can only say that God is faithful to all those who step out to serve Him.

Immediately following the Revolution there was such an outpouring of love for Romania and for the Romanian churches from Christians all over the world. Dozens of pastors came to visit us and encourage us in the Lord's work. We were overwhelmed by the kindness and love of these visitors, and God made them such a blessing to us.

One very meaningful visit that would have a long and lasting impact on my life and that of my family, on my ministry and the work of our church was that of a delegation of five pastors from Northern Ireland in February 1990, just two months after the events of Christmas 1989. The group was composed of Dr. Ian Paisley, Moderator of the Free Presbyterian Church of Ulster, a Member of the United Kingdom Parliament and a Member of the European Parliament, Dr. William McCrea, also a Member of the United Kingdom Parliament, Rev. Stanley Barnes, missionary Tom Lewis and Pastor Victor Maxwell.

The delegation had already been to Bucharest for preaching engagements before arriving in Timisoara. After they were shown around the city and the important sites of where the Revolution began, the pastors were delegated to preach in various churches. Our people were hungry for the Word of God, and when these men preached there was great blessing in the services, and many people came to faith in Jesus Christ. In truth, for us it was a spiritual revival.

While the other members of the delegation went to preach in other churches, Rev. Stanley Barnes and Victor Maxwell visited our church for the Wednesday night Bible study. During the days of communist rule Bethany Baptist had been an illegal underground church. We gathered in a simple meeting place, a modified house that belonged to a member of our church. With his consent we had knocked down some walls to accommodate the congregation. On that night I was able to translate for Stanley as he testified of what God had done in his life and then for Victor as he opened the Scriptures.

During that week we spent some time at the judicial trial of some former members of the secret police who had been charged with crimes against the people. We also took the delegation to visit several orphanages and hospitals, and then at the weekend they preached at churches in neighbouring towns and rural villages.

I remember that I spent most of that Sunday with Mr. Barnes, and as we talked I shared with him our hopes and plans for a proper church building and the things about which we were dreaming for the Lord's work in Romania.

That meeting with our brother cemented a bond that would bring great benefit and blessing to many for years to come.

Missionary Tom Lewis had arranged for that delegation from Northern Ireland to visit Romania after the late Pastor Doru Popa from Maranatha Baptist Church in Arad, Romania, paid a visit to Northern Ireland. Tom had been travelling into Romania for more than a decade, and through the years of the harsh and adverse conditions under communism, he had built up a very good relationship with all of these men of God.

The delegation arrived in Romania on a fact-finding mission to see what was happening in the newly liberated country and to visit the churches. The week was full of fellowship and friendship. There were meetings with political leaders, medical authorities and business managers. The main emphasis of the week was meeting with these pastors and their churches which were emerging out of decades of persecution and oppression. Many of the pastors were in awe of Dr. Paisley and were amazed at the liberty and authority with which he preached. They said that they were honoured to have such a man of this stature in their pulpits.

Stanley Barnes had requested of Tom Lewis that rather than accompany Dr. Paisley to all his services he would like to meet some of the pastors from the underground churches. It was in answer to this request that Tom arranged for Stanley and Victor to visit Bethany Baptist Church on that Wednesday night and to meet Pastor Eugen Groza.

In conversation with the two pastors Eugen explained the difficulties under which they had tried to function for several years. His was an underground church because it could not be registered with the government. Prior to the Revolution he was required every Monday morning to report to the police and inform them who had been speaking at their meetings. Even though this was a requirement, Eugen refused to conform to their demands and consequently, he suffered many interrogations

At the end of the delegation's visit to Romania all the visiting pastors were touched with the sincere gratitude these believers expressed, their humility in receiving foreign preachers so graciously and their obvious hunger for Christian fellowship and the preaching of the Word of God.

On leaving Romania the party took with them happy memories and lasting impressions, but Stanley Barnes also took with him a resolve to do something to help Pastor Eugen and his congregation at Bethany Baptist Church.

Stanley recalled the words of a preacher who summed up Christian compassion as, "A heart that has been dipped in the love of God." Stanley was sure that Eugen Groza had such a heart. His love for the Romanian people, the needy children and young people of the Timisoara region was unforgettable.

Stanley knew he had to do something.

Chapter 16

What Can We Do?

When he returned to his Hillsborough congregation Stanley Barnes was struck with the stark contrast between what he had witnessed in Romania and the quietness, order and prosperity of his local surroundings. He lost no time in relating to his church the details of what he had seen and experienced in Timisoara. Besides speaking of the social needs of the general population, Stanley also shared with them the testimony of how God had delivered this former Eastern Bloc country out of the grip of communism and how the Romanian Christian believers were rejoicing in their newfound freedoms. He specifically spoke of his visit to the former underground church and told something of the persecution they had passed through during Ceausescu's hard regime.

When he related to the Hillsborough people about Pastor Eugen, his family and the work at Bethany Baptist Church, it became evident to the congregation how much Stanley had been touched by the dedication and plight of this faithful servant of God. He spoke to them of the plainness and austerity of the building that was Bethany Baptist Church.

As Stanley transmitted this burden to his people he was heartened and encouraged to learn that they were not content just to learn of what had happened and to pray for Pastor Eugen and his church. They wanted to do something. They wanted to help Eugen and his family. The members at Hillsborough wanted to show solidarity with the believers at Bethany Baptist Church and assist them in a practical way.

In the autumn of 1990 Stanley invited Eugen to visit Northern Ireland for two weeks. It was very difficult for Romanians to obtain travel documents at that time, but Dr. Paisley was able to use his considerable influence to facilitate the necessary papers for Eugen, and very soon he was able to make the flights from Bucharest to Belfast.

During his time in Ulster Eugen was able to visit many Free Presbyterian churches and share with the people the burden that was on his heart for his own nation and especially for the people of Timisoara. Most Christians were anxious to learn firsthand of what had happened during the years of communist rule and how the believers and their Christian witness had survived. The Northern Ireland churches responded generously to these reports and each congregation Eugen visited gave unstintingly to help him return to Timisoara with substantial funds to support the work there

Eugen was able to stay at the Hillsborough manse with Stanley and Ina during his visit to Northern Ireland, and those two weeks further cemented the close bond that had already been created in Romania. Heather and Andrew, Stanley and Ina's children, listened keenly as Eugen spoke of his own family and shared about his experiences while living in communist Romania. What they heard from Eugen sounded so alien and strange from anything they had known in Northern Ireland's sheltered society.

Before leaving Ulster, Eugen insisted that Stanley make a return visit to Timisoara in 1991. After this invitation was graciously accepted Stanley and Ina with several friends from the church prepared for a trip to Romania. Besides gathering funds to take a sizeable gift with them for the Bethany Baptist Church, Stanley and the church organised for other people to contribute gifts to help with the social needs in Romania. Within a short time the friends at Hillsborough filled two large forty feet long container trucks with gifts of food, clothing, toys and medical supplies for Pastor Eugen to distribute among the needy people in Timisoara and the surrounding area. Michael Williamson and Gordon Martin gave freely of their time to drive those two loaded trucks across Europe to Timisoara.

Throughout the ten days they spent in Romania there were times of rich fellowship, visits to interesting sites and lots of fun and laughter as the two language groups of Romanian and Ulster believers tried to communicate with each other. This was an unforgettable experience for the Ulster visitors. However, a more lasting impression was yet to be made on the whole group.

Eugen organised for the party to travel from Timisoara to the small village of Recas to visit an orphanage where for a year Doru and Rodica Racovicean, two of Pastor Groza's colleagues, had been teaching the boys the Word of God and Christian music. There was both apprehension and anticipation about this trip, for so much had been reported in the media about Romania's orphans. The visitors were anxious to see the post-Revolution situation for themselves.

After the overthrow of Ceausescu in 1989, cameras captured horrific images for the Western media of the shocking conditions in which thousands of orphaned, abandoned and abused children were held in multiple, but inadequate institutions all over Romania. It must be said that most Romanians were also ignorant of the huge number of orphans and neglected children held in these appalling conditions until the revelations were made public after the Revolution. When the facts were eventually disclosed nearly all Romanians were thoroughly ashamed of how their government and social institutions had abused thousands of these boys and girls. It was a cause for national shame and concern.

During his dictatorial rule Ceausescu imposed harsh economic restrictions on his people, and this resulted in mass poverty. The majority of Romanians were living in considerable destitution. This fact, coupled with the poor social conditions of the country, made giving up one's offspring to a state-run orphanage an easy solution for many broken families. Under communism, abortions were outlawed. Ceausescu encouraged large families in order to increase the work force to produce more goods for the motherland. At the same time the Romanian government strictly controlled all fertility-regulation methods.

Against this background, many women gave birth to their so-called "illegitimate" children and were unable to care for them. Attempted abortions that went wrong resulted in high numbers of children born with special needs. Such children, as well as many with no evident problems, were abandoned to the care of the state. These pitiful children were crammed into ill-equipped state institutions where they were segregated by age and their perceived abilities or mental and physical handicaps.

These physically handicapped kids were kept apart from older and more able children. After periodic assessments many of the children and young people were labeled as "irrecoverable", and therefore, were allocated to virtual prisons with no normal resources whatsoever. They were incarcerated out of sight in drab institutions that looked more like human hencoops where food, clothing and heating were insufficient.

Worse still, these boys and girls were starved of affection, loving care, childish fun or any sound of laughter. Sometimes two and three infants were placed in a single steel cot. Many of these pitiful toddlers remained captive for the whole day in row after row of these metal cots, rocking back and forward while they made unintelligible noises.

A contributing factor to the deplorable plight of these children was the fact that the poorly paid staff was neither trained nor competent to meet the children's individual needs. Furthermore, no educational opportunity was provided for these unwanted orphaned and abandoned children. The outcome of all this was that the majority of these little ones were left with a very poor mental capacity, were emotionally highly strung and suffered from multiple behavioural problems.

Immediately following the Revolution, the cruel and dire conditions in which thousands of these poor children were held were exposed on television channels all over the world. There was a spontaneous outpouring of anger, shame, sympathy and offers to help. People wanted to do something. Foreign governments pledged financial help and charitable gifts; many agencies volunteered to adopt hundreds of these homeless children. Families in Europe, Australia and North America also offered to adopt these orphaned and ill-treated children.

Like other concerned people all over the world, the Hillsborough friends also heard about the plight of these deprived children and now that they were in Romania, they were desirous to see and meet some of these boys and girls. Pastor Eugen also wanted to take Stanley and his friends to see what the Romanian believers were doing to help alleviate the suffering of some of these little children.

When the Ulster group arrived in Recas, which is about twenty-three kilometres from Timisoara, they were taken to a state run orphanage where they were warmly received. They sat around the large dismal room, and very soon the group of between thirty to forty small boys, aged between four and twelve years, were paraded in to sing for the visitors. The visitors could not help but notice that the children were ill clad in old clothes, and their hair was shaved almost to the skin. Emotions were running high and tears coursed down many faces as the visitors looked on the children with great pity and compassion. Many of them were thinking of how well their own children and grandchildren were cared for back home in Northern Ireland while these precious little children were virtually destitute.

After singing in their native tongue and reciting several poems everyone present joined the boys as they lustily sang in English, "This is the day the Lord hath made…" The boys were thrilled to see they were fully understood so they tried another English chorus, "I will make you fishers of men…"

After the boys had finished singing there was a great round of spontaneous applause from the visiting friends.   When given permission to mingle with the visiting friends the boys were absolutely euphoric.   They started hugging the foreigners, touching their skin and clothes while chattering in their native tongue.   They wanted to look through the cameras and have their photos taken.   It was obvious that they craved personal attention, and the visitors were happy to hug them in return and pour their hearts out in love and affection for the children.   Each one of these boys once had a father and a mother, but they had been left destitute without ever knowing a parent's smile, a father's hug or the warmth of a mother's love.

The visit to the orphanage went by very quickly, and soon it was time to return to Timisoara.   Before the group left the children sang for them again and asked them to come back and visit them on another occasion.   One tiny lad came over to Stanley, clasped his little hand into Stanley's and looked up at him with large brown eyes asking, "Would you be my daddy?"

Stanley was so deeply touched by this heart-rending request, his eyes swelled with tears and his heart with pity for this little boy.

Later Eugen explained to the visitors that this small group of children was only a drop in the bucket of an estimated 100,000 boys and girls in Romania's institutions and this was one of the sad legacies that godless communism had bequeathed to them.   He appealed to them all for their prayers for Romania's abandoned children.

Stanley and Ina had taken the group from Northern Ireland to Romania to help and encourage Pastor Eugen and the friends at Bethany Baptist Church.   However, having heard the children sing and seen their situation, they returned home challenged and determined to do something to try and alleviate the pitiful conditions of the children of Recas.

Chapter 17

Who Cares for the Abused and Abandoned?

Stanley and Ina carried heavy hearts as they returned from their visit to Recâs. They knew that everyone else on the trip shared the same burden and heartache for the little lads they had met in the orphanage. Their sweet and enthusiastic singing had given much pleasure to the visitors, but the thought of them returning to their long meal tables and cold dormitories without the love of a mother and father or the prospect of any hopeful future weighed heavily on their hearts.

Pastor Eugen was so encouraged by Stanley's proposal that he and the Hillsborough Church would endeavour to do something practical for these children. Stanley had the confidence that his congregation back home would show the same outpouring of love on these abused children as the rest of the group.

No sooner had Stanley mentioned his laudable suggestion when Eugen tempered it by a cautionary word. He explained that another church group had accompanied him on a visit to the same orphanage several months earlier and they also were greatly moved by what they had seen. They took hundreds of photos and shot lots of movies to show to their friends back home. Before leaving the orphanage the group leader pledged to Eugen that they would organise for the children to visit their country and raise support for their welfare.

When the children heard of the visitor's promise they got really excited at the prospect of going on a foreign trip. For months afterwards they waited in the hope of hearing from those friends about the promised help and trip. Sadly, no invitation ever arrived nor did Eugen ever hear from the group or the leader again. Worse still, the children were devastated, for they had been sure these people would bring a little happiness and excitement into their lives.

In the light of this disappointment Stanley spoke to Eugen of the possibility of inviting the children to visit Northern Ireland. Eugen readily agreed but also agreed with Stanley that it would be wiser not to say anything about it until he had spoken to his elders and committee at Hillsborough. Stanley had no doubts that his office bearers and congregation would give their whole-hearted support for the proposed visit.

At this Eugen almost wept for joy. Stanley promised that all expenses for the whole party would be fully covered and that they would give the boys an unforgettable holiday. He would also arrange a series of meetings at which the boys would sing in Romanian and English and then Eugen would speak about his work and the needs for special care for these children. In this way they would try to raise funds for the furtherance of their work in Timisoara.

On arrival back home in Hillsborough Stanley disclosed to his Clerk of Session, David Williamson, the proposed arrangement he had made with Eugen inviting the disadvantaged boys from the Recâs orphanage to be their guests in Hillsborough for two weeks. David was full of enthusiasm when he heard the news and immediately gave his unreserved support to the project.

Stanley and David took the proposal to the church session, and after a short discussion it was unanimously approved. Very soon the whole church at Hillsborough was buzzing with excitement as they made plans to host forty boys and their supervisors on the church property. They had been shocked at the sad images they had seen on television of the thousands of homeless children in Romania. They were also moved at the firsthand reports Stanley and other members of the group had given to the church. Now they had an opportunity to do something practical to help.

Preparation for the upcoming visit was planned with the precision of a military manoeuvre. Kind people provided an abundance of everything that was needed; beds, sleeping bags, sheets, pillows, toiletries, clothes, shoes, lots of toys and an abundance of food and confectionery. The young visitors would lack for nothing. Friends from inside and outside the church membership made generous monetary donations that were given to help with expenses. Ina drew up a rota for those who had volunteered for catering and cleaning. Stanley and David Williamson put their heads together to plan out the programme and itinerary for the two weeks with an equal balance of deputation meetings, excursions to places of interest and visits to recreational attractions.

When Eugen and Mihaela arrived with the children and their supervisors the Hillsborough people gave them such a royal welcome that the children were quite overwhelmed. Not only had they never been outside Romania, they had never known what it was to have such sincere love and attention showered on them. The ladies of the congregation who had prepared a welcome meal for the group could not hold back the tears.

Over the next two weeks the Hillsborough church building reverberated with laughter, singing, chatter and shouts as the children played their games, enjoyed their meals and had their devotions.

Stanley accompanied Pastor Groza and the boys' choir to all the meetings in various Free Presbyterian Churches. News of "A Romanian Orphan Boys Choir" was a massive attraction to Northern Ireland's Christian public, and night after night the children sang for large gatherings. Pastor Groza followed by telling of his work and related how the children kept asking him why these people were doing all this. They wanted to know why did they show such love towards them? Eugene said that he had explained to the children that it was because they loved the Saviour and therefore, they wanted to show His love towards them.

Besides the church meetings, a luxury coach transported the Romanian group to visit the beautiful Antrim Coast Road, Ulster's principal attraction, the Giants Causeway, the American folk Museum near Omagh and many ice cream shops along the way.

When the two weeks were over there were lots of hugs and an abundance of tears as the hosts and guests exchanged their farewells before the children left Ulster for Romania. The children and the team of workers who had accompanied them were totally astounded by the love, kindness and generosity that had been shown to them. They would never forget their first visit outside their homeland, and understandably, they wanted to return to Northern Ireland on another day.

This visit by the boys from Recas was followed later by a visit from the girls from the orphanage in Lugoj. Perhaps the highlight of that visit was the civic reception banquet at Belfast's magnificent City Hall when the Lord Mayor, Sir Reg Empey, hosted the children and their team of helpers. The banquet was attended by leading politicians including Dr. and Mrs. Paisley and Dr. William McCrea. It was a memorable night when the sweet voices of those children reverberated from the domed ceiling of the majestic banquet hall.

Eugen and his cousin, Pastor Petru Dugulescu, who was pastor at the First Baptist Church in Timisoara, shared a common vision of forming an evangelistic association to help promote a moral and spiritual awakening in Romania. Like many other pastors, Petru had also suffered immense persecution from the dreaded Securitate, and on one occasion was nearly killed in what appeared to be a set up "automobile accident". Such planned tragedies were not uncommon during the communist years.

The outcome of Petru and Eugen's shared vision in 1991 was to organise a Timisoara based missionary agency, "Isus Speranta Romaniei" – "Jesus Hope of Romania" (ISR). Their aim was to organise biblical symposiums, theological seminars and other avenues to encourage Romanian Christian workers.

Shortly after the formation of ISR, Petru Dugulescu stood as a candidate for the Romanian parliament and was successfully returned as a parliamentarian to represent a district of Timisoara. With Petru having to devote so much time to his political activities, Eugen concentrated on leading the ministry and building a good team of spiritual and gifted men around him. Their combined gifts were multiple and complemented each other in that expanding ministry.

Another one of their aims through the ISR mission was to provide social help to disadvantaged families and a secure home for some of the needy and ill-treated children in Timisoara. It was with this in mind that, early in the life of ISR, the board set up the Onesimus Christian Home for Boys to be a shelter for many young boys who had been left homeless on the streets of Timisoara.

This venture presented the team with a dilemma and a challenge. They discovered that the more they tried to provide sanctuary for these children the more they found that the need to help Romania's children was even greater than what they had first thought. This challenge was answered by taking the matter to God in prayer. The answer came when they discerned that God had other plans ahead.

After hearing about the formation of ISR mission and the Onesimus Christian Home for Boys, Stanley and his church session arranged to host another group of underprivileged Romanian boys at their Hillsborough Church. As on the previous visits, the members at Hillsborough Free Presbyterian Church, threw in all their weight as they welcomed and cared for these boys during their two weeks in Northern Ireland. For the children, it was like heaven on earth. The sun shone on them as they toured around Ulster's countryside and regions of outstanding beauty. They had fun at crazy golf, go-karting and bowling. As on the previous visit, Free Presbyterian churches across Ulster prepared lavish suppers for these children after they sang at the church services. The whole Romanian party made many friends at the Hillsborough church, and at the end of the tour they were reluctant to leave Northern Ireland to return to Timisoara.

Eugen used his visit to Northern Ireland with the boys from the Onesimus Christian Home for Boys to speak at all the meetings of the progress of his work in Romania, the establishing of the "Jesus Hope of Romania" mission, the opening of this home for boys and his work at Bethany Baptist Church in Timisoara. The churches responded again with their pronounced generosity to help with the various areas of the growing work of the ISR mission and the Bethany Church.

Chapter 18

Blessings at Bethany

Many preachers from all over Europe and the United States of America arrived in Timisoara to see the aftermath of the Revolution and offer help to churches and social institutions. While some came with cameras to make movies and documentaries, others came with an offer of genuine help for the people. They were overwhelmed with the needs, both social and spiritual.

In the aftermath of the revolution Romania suffered from a deep economic depression. There were shortages of food and medical supplies. Hospitals were ill equipped; shops were bereft of daily provisions and general clothing; many children were living in orphanages without sufficient food or care, and church buildings were in disrepair. The needs were so crushing and overwhelming that most visitors did not know where to start.

It was obvious to all that it would take decades to help these people, and the most effective way would be by building trustworthy relationships between Romanians and people outside Romania, between churches in Romania and believers in other countries. There were no great and grandiose answers to the monumental social, material and spiritual problems of this country. Little by little and step by step progress could be made.

While other churches had had their proper buildings, this was not the case at Bethany Baptist. Because of their illegal status they had occupied the house that was kindly granted to them for their meetings. By the time of the Revolution the Bethany Baptist congregation had grown from its original seventy-three members to 240. During the eleven years of its existence Bethany Baptist had survived the restrictive communist rule. Throughout that time they had been opposed, persecuted, ostracised, robbed and the building frequently stoned. On one occasion after the building had been broken into and musical instruments stolen, complaints were made to the local authorities. The reply they got was dismissive and insulting, "Go and ask your God who did it, and maybe He will find them."

In 1990 Bethany Baptist extended an invitation to Eugen Groza to become the first pastor of the church. This is a position that he had almost grown into. Since his return to Timisoara in 1983 Eugen and Mihaela had been a vital part of the church. As he had opportunity he ministered the Word of God in the congregation and during his critical illness in 1987 the fellowship surrounded Eugen and his family with their love and prayers. Eugen was ordained as pastor of Bethany Baptist Church on 2nd December 1990.

Eugen was not only the first pastor to be installed at Bethany Baptist Church this was his first pastorate and would be his only pastorate. Pastoral ministry is very similar to swimming in that a person can only learn to swim by swimming. Eugen had much to learn as a pastor when he took on the awesome responsibility as the leader of this large church. He was grateful for the mature and spiritual elders the Lord had provided around him at the Bethany Church. All of them made a significant contribution to the fellowship of the church and to Eugen's life.

The oldest of these elders were Pavel Pobega and Vasile Sâtnic. They were spiritual giants and their guidance and help to Pastor Eugen were invaluable. They taught the young pastor how to care for others and give them counsel. They were wise in their guidance, and the Lord gave Eugen the humility to learn and benefit from these faithful men.

Immediately following the Revolution Bethany Baptist was registered as a legal church and subsequently they no longer suffered the opposition to which they had become so accustomed.

Although the communist regime tried, it could not stop the growth of the congregation. As the congregation increased the leaders had to knock down walls to augment the capacity of the building. With the surge in the number of people attending churches early in 1990 there were no more walls to knock down at Bethany Baptist Church or room to enlarge the building.

The bond that was established between Eugen and Stanley helped bring about a solution to this problem. Locally, the Timisoara City Hall leased a derelict site at 22 Ion Barac Street to the members at Bethany Baptist for their new church. However, with the congregation materially impoverished, they needed outside help.

Pastor Eugen invited Stanley to accompany him to view the dilapidated site. A few old pieces of rusted machinery littered the allotment which was heavily overgrown with weeds. Eugen enlarged on his plans and hopes of what they would like to build as a testimony to the Gospel of the Lord Jesus Christ. As they stood surveying the spot Stanley put his hand on Eugen's shoulder and said, "Brother Eugen, let's have a word of prayer to commit this project to the Lord and by faith lift an offering in heaven."

Stanley encouraged Eugen to take a step of faith and make a start to build the new church. Having already been involved in two building programmes back home in Hillsborough, Stanley had proved the words of Hudson Taylor who said "God's work done God's way will never lack God's support".

Stanley also covenanted with Eugene that he would seek to raise support in Northern Ireland to help with the construction of this new church. The two men bowed their heads and prayed to Almighty God for His provision and direction.

As news of this need filtered out to other Free Presbyterian congregations and individuals, gifts began to flow into the Romanian Fund that the Hillsborough Church had established. They were glad to channel these generous donations to the friends at Bethany Baptist who transformed the monetary gifts into bricks and mortar to erect their new building.

During the course of the building programme, Michael Williamson, Gordon Martin, Edward Heron and Ken Agnew made several overland trips to Romania in large container trucks filled with materials and machinery to help with the construction programme. This cooperation greatly enhanced the progress of the building and further strengthened the bond of fellowship between Bethany Baptist and the congregation of Hillsborough.

Within eighteen months the new church building was ready. However, in the course of the construction tragedy visited the Bethany Baptist congregation. While Eugen was away preaching in another part of Romania, Emanuel, the son of Isaia and Viorica Tamas, was painting the interior of the building which was nearing completion. Isaia was one of the church deacons, and he was largely responsible for the construction of the new building. It is still unclear how the tragedy happened, but it seems that the paint Emanuel was using was too near an open gas fire. The combination of fumes and open flame caused combustion and this resulted in a terrible explosion. Young Emanuel suffered severe burns over 90% of his body, and sadly, he survived for only a few days. Eugen had to rush back to Timisoara to help comfort the family and then conduct a very sad funeral service.

The beautiful completed church building was a tribute to Isaia's diligence and dedication as the builder. It was somewhat ironic that the new Bethany Church should be crowned as a final homage and epitaph to the memory of his son, Emanuel.

The new church building was nearing completion and all the members were looking forward to the day when they would transfer from the renovated and enlarged house to this new structure. Eugen had already invited Stanley to return to Romania and honour them by preaching at the opening of their new sanctuary. Not only did Stanley travel to Romania, but sixty-three friends from various Free Presbyterian Churches accompanied him for this special occasion.

In a pamphlet prepared for the opening of their beautiful new structure on 18th September 1994, the leadership at Bethany Baptist Church told their story in their own words:

> Looking back we can see grace, plenty of grace poured over "Bethany" Church by God: that is why we say together with the psalmist: "Not unto us, Lord, not to us, but to your name be the glory."

> "Bethany" was born as an answer to the struggle in prayer from a group of believers from Timisoara, most of whom were members of the First Baptist Church and their strong desire to serve God and the people. Looking directly unto the Lord Jesus Christ, Who is the Head of the Church, while they were facing all kinds of threatening and prohibitions from the communist power of that time, they felt the urgent need of spiritual renewal for society. With an understanding of the mission of the church in the world, a group of believers, full of courage and faith based on the power of God, decided to form a church, another house of prayer in Timisoara. They called it "Bethany" as they wanted with all their hearts for everyone to know that Jesus Christ was their Lord forever.

> Bethany has been a warm and living church, prayerful and hospitable, a place where people have been able to drop their burdens, and many lives have been changed through the power of God.

> After much searching, a building was found at 2 Comuna din de Paris Street. Officially, a new church could not be started, so the building was bought in the names of the families, Toader and Gruescu. That house served as a temple for the congregation since then until today.

The original group of leaders who took the initiative was composed: Petru Gruescu, Vasile Sâtnic, Nicolae Toader and Vasile Ianculovici. The official opening of the church took place on 18th November 1979. Brothers Pavel Pobega and Vasile Sâtnic were the first deacons of the church and the first speaker was Brother Pavel Pobega. The first guest preacher in the pulpit was Brother Cure. At the beginning of the weekly church programme the services were conducted only on Fridays and Saturdays.

Guided by the Holy Spirit and under the leadership of the two deacons, Pavel Pobega and Vasile Sâtnic, the church started to grow in number and maturity so that we commenced regular worship services. The first committee was: Pavel Pobega–deacon, Nicolae Toader–Secretary (Clerk of Session) and Petru Gruescu–Treasurer.

In 1980 the church had its first choir with Brother Petru Gruescu as the music conductor. At the same time we founded the church orchestra which at the beginning consisted almost only of the Iancu family. The father, Ion Iancu, was the leader of the orchestra.

Bethany had many enemies for whom we have prayed, and we continue to pray for them. Many times stones were thrown at the church and windows broken; musical items and audio equipment were stolen. When we complained to the authorities their response was, "Ask your God to find those who have done it." Many times we were fined without any good reason. But what could these people do to us? God has been with us; the church has grown; our enemies have been knocked down, and in this new liberty, paid for by the precious blood of many young people from Timisoara, for the first time the church had the opportunity to choose a pastor.

In 1990 brother Eugen Groza was chosen and ordained as the first pastor in the history of this church, and in 1992 brother Teofil Ciortuz was ordained as the second pastor.

Three years ago, in 1991, after much thought and prayer, we began the great adventure of raising a new building for our church. That which seemed to be a dream in the beginning has now become a reality. God has blessed us more than we could have imagined, and today the building is ready to be dedicated for the service of God.

Within a short while the friends at Bethany Baptist founded two more daughter congregations which now stand on their own feet as Baptist churches. Six other Baptist churches have also been planted in the greater Timisoara area. Bethany Baptist congregation also purchased the property adjacent to the church which was opened as a kindergarten and a youth centre.

Even though the visitors from Northern Ireland could not understand the Romanian language, they were richly blessed in meeting these sincere and humble believers and joining in their worship and celebrations. David Williamson, Clerk of Session at Hillsborough Free Presbyterian Church, speaking at the opening of the new church on behalf of the Free Presbyterian Churches of Ulster, gave greetings to the large congregation.

The large number of visitors from Ulster formed an impromptu choir and sang a hymn of praise in English. Rev. Stanley Barnes gave the main address in which he preached on a phrase that was used of John the Baptist, "He shall be great in the sight of the Lord" (Luke 1:15).

This trip to Romania undergirded the fellowship that had already been well established between Bethany Baptist Church and the Free Presbyterian Churches of Ulster and also between these two men of God, Pastor Eugen Groza and Rev. Stanley Barnes.

Nevertheless, there was more to see, and an even deeper and more lasting impression would be made on these visitors to Romania.

Chapter 19

And Still There is More

Stanley returned to Romania for another visit in 1998. While there Eugen introduced him to Lorena Rusovan who was the director of Onesimus Christian Home for Boys. Stanley was amazed as Lorena took time to tell him of what the Lord had done in her life and through her ministry.

Lorena had been born to Christian parents in a small mining town on the banks of the River Danube near the Romanian border with Serbia. Her grandfather was a pastor who travelled by bicycle over the hills to meet up with isolated believers in small village churches.

When Lorena was only two months old Ceausescu swept to power in Bucharest. She recalled that throughout her childhood her grandfather and parents were often harassed and persecuted for being Christians. Lorena remembers the day when she was twelve years old that the Securitate raided her home. They ransacked her father's office and overturned all the bookshelves in his library in their pursuit to find and confiscate Bibles and Christian books.

As a little girl Lorena could not understand why her dad often spent hours in the basement of their house. It was only later that she learned that it was there that he studied the Bible and secretly listened to radio broadcasts from the BBC, Radio Free Europe and several other Christian radio stations.

Lorena's dad was the financial manager of a local mining company.

When it came to the attention of the Securitate that he was a Christian believer they made life very difficult for him. To retain his job he had to avoid regularly attending the evangelical church in their town. Instead, on Sundays he travelled out of town to worship at a village church; therefore, he was less exposed to the attention of the Securitate.

Meanwhile, Lorena's mother continued to take Lorena and her brother to the family church, which was four kilometres away. Kind neighbours offered Lorena's family a ride each Sunday on their horse-drawn carriage to the church and this was great fun for her and her brother.

Lorena progressed well through her school years. On the day after she had finished her high school exams and gained entrance to university in August 1983, she was involved in a serious accident. While riding her bicycle near her home a car struck her. The vehicle drove on and left the young girl injured at the side of the road. A passerby found her and took Lorena to hospital where she was operated on for a very bad compound fracture. During the next three years Lorena was subjected to another six operations, and during that time she was not able to walk. Consequently, she was not able to accept her place at university as had been planned.

During those prolonged months when she was confined to bed Lorena had plenty of time to think, read and pray. Her dad kept her supplied with a good range of Christian classics including the works of C. S. Lewis and Charles Spurgeon's sermons. All of these books were photocopies of an original. They helped her to seriously reflect on her own personal relationship with Jesus Christ. It was during those days that she was glad that she was a Christian and had the assurance of Christ's presence in her heart.

In the spring of 1985, when Lorena was twenty years old, she had her sixth operation. After the surgery her doctor told her that there was little chance that she would ever be able to walk again. At first she was shattered with this devastating news, but through her tears she realised that despite this apparent setback, God had a plan for her life. With this assurance she earnestly prayed that God would not leave her confined to a bed for the rest of her life.

While she was still suffering from the repeated operations Lorena applied for admittance to university on the strength of her success with her entrance exams three years earlier. She was overjoyed when she received notice that she had been awarded a place at the University of Timisoara. When she began her studies she was still walking awkwardly with the aid of two walking sticks because she was not able to obtain a wheelchair.

While she was a student at university an opportunity arose for students to go on a school trip to Poland to visit the Nazi concentration camps. Lorena had studied all about World War II and was keen to be included in the group going to Poland. When the names of those going were disclosed she could not understand for what reason she had not been included.

Back home she cried to her parents because she had been turned down without any good reason. It was then that her dad sat down with her and explained that it was because her family was perceived by the Securitate to be Christian believers. He told her that for that reason she should not to be surprised that she would be denied and deprived of certain privileges that other students enjoyed. Her wise father went on to explain that the Securitate kept a file on each person, and it would be noted in hers that she was a pastor's granddaughter and her parents were believers. He said that this would always be held against her and it was part of the price they paid for being Christians. That prolonged talk with her dad helped Lorena put things into perspective.

Very soon Lorena made new friends far from home in Timisoara and was thrilled to find out that some of them were also Christian believers. They invited her to go with them to a house where they regularly attended for Bible study. Lorena soon discovered that this was the meeting place of underground Bethany Baptist Church.

Photographic Section

Strawberry picking at Deborah House

Visiting the children at Recas

Be My Daddy

Photo Section

Deborah girls at farewell Service Hillsborough 2012

Be My Daddy

Visit to Martyrs Memorial

Dr. McCrea congratulates Pastor Groza on receiving his Doctorate

First Deborah House

Parents of Deborah House I & II

Be My Daddy

Deborah House 2

Part of team who insulated and replastered the Deborah House I

Photo Section

Lorena with husband Daniel and son Paul

Nico and Florica Toader

Be My Daddy

Emil, Adriana, Melissa and Evelyn Toader

Little John and his wife Elana

Photo Section

Doru & Rodica Racovicean

Stanley and Eugen relaxing!

Eugen and Mihaela with their family

Photo Section

Visit to Deborah House I 2008

Armagh Church Group 2012.

Ballymoney Church Group 2013

Be My Daddy

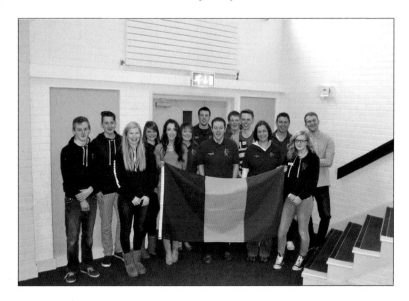

Portadown Reach Team 2014

Distributing Bibles at Buzias Rehabilation Centre

Portavogie Church Group 2013

Portavogie outreach team with the boys at Buzias Young Offenders

These fellowship meetings with like-minded students sustained Lorena through her university days until she finally graduated. Providentially, Lorena's graduation corresponded with the aftermath of the Romanian Revolution, and that changed the whole atmosphere in the nation.

After the completion of her university studies Lorena secured an excellent job in the new Romania with the Ammon Electrical Engineering firm in Timisoara. She had the particular responsibility of designing electrical power plants. Lorena enjoyed this responsible position in the engineering company and also was very happy to continue to worship at Bethany Baptist Church where Pastor Eugen Groza ministered the Word of God.

After two years in her engineering job Pastor Eugen introduced Lorena to the work of Onesimus Christian Home for Boys and asked her if she would consider becoming a full-time worker with this agency. At first, Lorena discounted the very thought of giving up her good and promising career to take up a lowly and menial position in a boys' home for street children. She felt that nothing could have been further from her thoughts. At the same time, she knew that she dared not share these views with Pastor Groza who was so dedicated to his work. However, to satisfy the pastor's serious conversation she assured him she would be praying about his suggestion.

Although Lorena tried to set aside the pastor's invitation she did not have any peace about it nor could she get the matter out of her mind. One night in May 1992 Lorena had a dream in which she was attending a meeting in her hometown church. She did not recognise the preacher, but listened intently as he said, "If you need to make a decision you must do what Saul did on the Damascus Road: fall before the Lord and cry, 'Lord what wilt Thou have me to do?'"

Lorena woke up from her dream quite startled for she felt God had spoken to her in the night. She started to look in her Bible to read what happened to Paul after he made that prayer of surrender. What she read arrested her attention even more: "The Lord said, 'Arise and go into the city and it shall be told you what you shall do.'" Although she tried to get over to sleep again that early morning, her sleep just would not return.

The next morning, without any further equivocation, Lorena went to her office, wrote her resignation from the engineering company and submitted it to her manager. He was taken aback and asked, "Do you know what you are doing?" Lorena assured him that she did know what this meant.

Following her sudden resignation Lorena phoned Pastor Eugen and asked if he was still looking for someone to fill the vacancy at the Onesimus Christian Home for Boys. When he replied in the affirmative she related to him what had happened, how she had just submitted her resignation from the company and was available to work at the home.

To give up a prestigious job that had given her immense satisfaction and promised a secure and prosperous future, in order to work among deprived street kids was a big step, but Lorena had no regrets. She knew that this was what God wanted her to do and she was happy to step out of that secular position to serve Him.

It might be asked of Lorena, "What were the future prospects for this work?"

God had the answer.

Chapter 20

As Busy as a Bee

When the anti-communist Revolution occurred in Romania in December 1989, there was universal outrage when it was discovered that scores of boys and girls were sleeping on the streets of Timisoara. These ill clad and filthy children and young people were often aggressive to each other, and they were a menace to the general public of Timisoara. However, it was also perceived that they were the result of an abusive and tyrannical system of neglect in which such abuse was allowed to happen.

Under the communist regime parents could beat their child to death with no fear of retribution because there was no law to protect children against violence from their own parents. Under the same system, incredibly, a mother could leave the maternity hospital and not take her baby home with her. Sadly, an abandoned or abused child was nothing more than a name to be registered on a file, and afterwards that little one was incarcerated in some obscure and dismal institution.

Even after the Revolution of 1989, it was estimated that every year more than eleven thousand children were victims of abuse in Romania, and less than one per cent of these benefited from any post-trauma assistance.

Lorena settled very quickly into her position at the Onesimus Christian Home for Boys and soon assumed the role of director for the agency which was a branch of the "Jesus Hope of Romania" mission. From the first day she took a personal interest in each boy and tried to understand his problems and improve his situation. Little by little she got to know the boys, and they in turn gained increasing trust in her compassionate concern for them.

This first responsibility of caring for delinquent children was only a step to a wider ministry that would soon open for Lorena. One day she was searching in a nearby village for information she needed to locate the birth record for an orphan boy. The information about this boy was necessary in order to obtain his national identity card. During that search, Lorena got involved in rescuing an orphaned six-year-old girl from sexual and physical abuse at the hands of strangers. Because of the lack of child abuse laws, cultural indifference and disinterested police in the village, the girl's rescue was difficult and complicated.

Even though Lorena objected to the girl's heartbreaking circumstances and despite the fact that she had been physically harmed and was psychologically traumatised, the girl was officially classified as being "retarded". Consequently, the victimised child was put into a government orphanage with over 250 other children aged between five years and eighteen years with only five full-time care workers and no individual attention or therapy.

The incident, in which Lorena encountered this young victim of sexual abuse caused her to focus her attention on the fact that there were no alternatives available for this little girl or any other of the many abused girls on the streets of Timisoara. There was no residential care or treatment for them or help for their behavioural disorders.

These molested and underage girls frequently became involved in prostitution and thieving - mostly to obtain money to buy food. Bereft of normal family life, they were reared with incomprehensible emotional and behavioural problems. Yet, such girls are part of God's creation. Lorena tried to imagine how she would feel if one of these girls had been her daughter. She felt that no one had the right to judge these girls for what a sick and sinful society had done to them. As a concerned Christian she knew that she and her friends at Bethany Baptist Church had the moral responsibility to show these disadvantaged girls that God loves them and how special and important they are to Him.

The circumstances of that six-year-old abused girl, who Lorena had come across in the course of searching for a boy's registration, had shocked her. She knew that what she had witnessed should be totally unacceptable for her society. It was this that motivated Lorena to speak with Pastor Groza and convince him that something needed to be done for such neglected and abused girls.

Eugen was moved as he listened to Lorena. He also felt he had to do something in view of this stressful dilemma. Besides praying about the matter and trusting God to open a way for them, Eugen also knew that his friends in Northern Ireland and the United States would want to share in this burden.

Once again the people at Hillsborough responded immediately with great enthusiasm and generosity. Stanley invited Pastor Eugen for two weeks of deputation meetings in Free Presbyterian churches to share this new vision, burden and challenge of providing a new Christian home for these abused girls.

Eugen was also able to communicate his vision to his friends in the United States with whom he had been cooperating in the Missio Link International Foundation (MLI). The MLI, of which Eugen is the president, consists of a mission board with members in Romania and the USA. This Christian body is committed to addressing the material and spiritual needs of the Romanians through a variety of ministry initiatives including their concern and work amongst these needy and abused children. At the heart of this mission is a Romanian team of uniquely equipped servants of God: Eugen Groza, Emil Toader, Lorena Rusovan, Ion Costache, Doru Racovicean and Florin Iosub.

Teamwork was essential to be able to fulfil the aims for which MLI had been created. Amongst others, Nico Toader had always been an enormous help and encouragement to Eugen since the foundation of the Bethany Church and in all the different outreach ministries of MLI. Nico was a big man, a gentle giant with a big heart of love for his Lord and for the Lord's people. He was also a gifted elder at the church whose example touched everyone. Later he was ordained as a pastor by the Bethany congregation to care for two village churches in Lenauheim and Graba. These small churches had been planted through the outreach programme of Bethany Baptist Church. Nico remained faithful to his charge and call to the ministry until the Lord called him home.

His son, Pastor Emil Toader, followed in his father's footsteps and stood by Eugen in the youth ministry at Bethany Baptist. Later, he became a member of the original board of MLI. Emil also studied for two years at Belfast Bible College and afterwards did extra studies at London University. Today he is pastoring the Holy Trinity Baptist Church in Timisoara. Besides his pastoral ministry, Emil also leads the mountain youth camp programme for MLI which is known as Alpiniş. This ministry is dedicated to reaching and equipping the younger generation in Romania with the Gospel through camps, outdoor activities and spiritual retreats.

These camps are located in the mountains near Sibiu where Alpiniş has a conference centre that they use for Christian outreach, discipleship training and leadership development. Every year hundreds of young and older Romanians attend these camps and conferences.

Determined to establish a Christ-centred programme for Romania, Lorena persuaded the MLI Foundation to help them open a home for the protection and healing of severely traumatised girls. As God provided adequate funds through the generosity of His people, Pastor Eugen and Lorena were able to secure an old dilapidated property. This building had to undergo extensive renovations and refurbishment to transform it into a suitable structure.

Teams of workers, including Clarke Hill and David Millar from Cookstown, descended on the property to fully renovate this old building. David owns a local tool company and is director of Lafarge Cement. They were accompanied by a group of young men from Hillsborough Free Church and Cookstown Baptist. A dentist and a teacher also formed part of the party. Added to this contingent the local people in the Cookstown area raised the sum of £31,000.00 for the project.

The new unit was opened in May 2002 and it was aptly named, "Deborah House Centre". Deborah is the only female prophet of the Old Testament and her name means "as busy as a bee". That summed up the work of the home and especially the role played by Lorena. She was not only the founder but also the first director of Deborah House, and this was very much a hands-on job.

Right from the start Lorena was there with Eugen and other friends when they purchased the old dwelling for this new ministry. After that Lorena supervised the renovation of the building to make it suitable for the requirements of the home. Added to this she also had to equip the new unit with furnishings, bedding, kitchen and laundry equipment and administrative office apparatus. Afterwards Lorena had to recruit and interview all the suitable staff: the house parents, the counsellors, the social worker, the carers and the kitchen staff.

Finally, Lorena sought out the neediest girls in Timisoara, and one-by-one introduced them to the new ambience of a Christian home where they would be loved and cared for. It was a mammoth task, but the Lord helped her even as He had promised. These abandoned and abused girls were rescued from all sorts of horrible backgrounds and individually admitted to Deborah House. The girls were carefully assessed and their particular needs were addressed. In time forty girls were introduced to the care of Lorena and her staff.

The Deborah House Centre was unique in Romania from its inception. This sanctuary was designed to provide a safe shelter from a traumatic past; it was also a Christian home environment where these girls would feel loved and cared for. Lorena wanted it to be a unique refuge for severely abused girls where they could be provided with healing for all of their hurts so that each girl would be able to reclaim her life from being under the shadow of her abuser or abusers. To do this Lorena designed a programme to assess and treat the physical and sexual abuse and other related behavioural disorders which these girls might have suffered.

When they arrived at Deborah House the girls were admitted with their complex and chronic post-traumatic psychological problems. Many of them had experienced sexual and physical abuse from a very young age and consequently, suffered from intense fear, nightmares and agitated behaviour. Some of them arrived in such a debilitated state of suffering from serious injury that their very lives were in jeopardy.

The express purpose of the home was to offer rescue, sanctuary, therapy, counselling, education and hope in a Christian home environment. Lorena's goal was that each girl would be able to reclaim her life from under the shadow of her abuser. The Centre also served the entire community, including Rroma (gypsy) girls who faced the additional obstacle of ethnic discrimination in Romania.

Lorena did not forget the six-year-old girl she rescued in 1998. As a result of her persistence, the young child was eventually transferred from the "retarded" section of a government orphanage to Deborah House. After a year of intensive therapy and vital skilled social counselling, she was able to attend school. In her second school year at Deborah House she took first place in her mathematics class. That girl was the original inspiration for Deborah House coming into being, and today she continues to demonstrate the success of Lorena's inspirational programme by her remarkable recovery.

Deborah House has been successful in implementing post-trauma treatment programmes for these abused girls. These programmes are unique in Romania. Besides providing residential care, Lorena and her staff assess and treat the girls for physical and sexual abuse and other related behavioural disorders. The staff is also available to provide individual attention, counselling and tutoring in school, work and vital social skills. They also endeavour to empower the girls to return to society, and the Deborah House staff has demonstrated a remarkable ability to use their resources wisely and efficiently.

Lorena and the leadership around her entered into a close working relationship with the local Romanian authorities, including the Timis County Agency for Child Protection. In recognition of its importance as a model programme Deborah House was awarded grants from several prestigious organisations within Romania.

Not long after the new Deborah House was inaugurated Stanley Barnes extended yet another invitation to Pastor Groza and Lorena to organise the girls into a choir and plan a visit to Northern Ireland. As usual the congregation at Hillsborough rose to the occasion and did an excellent job of looking after both the girls and the staff members who came with them. However, on this occasion, they had to prepare for an invasion of young girls from abused backgrounds. Some of the Deborah House staff and their families planned to accompany the girls. For the Hillsborough people it was a gigantic undertaking, but, as on the previous occasions, they provided them with the very best of hospitality.

When the girls and the staff finally arrived they were overwhelmed. They had never seen such an abundance of everything they needed. Again a full programme was organised and the choir-girls toured all over Ulster, visited recreational centres and were royally welcomed to each church they visited. Their singing was such a blessing, and the congregations could hardly believe that the girls had come from such a difficult background. At each meeting Lorena thanked the people for their support and generosity that made the ministry of Deborah House possible. Night after night Pastor Eugen presented the challenge from the Word of God.

The churches again demonstrated their generosity in sending the Deborah House party back to Romania with an abundance of gifts to help maintain and further their great work.

For five years Lorena continued to work alongside Pastor Eugen as Director of the Deborah House Centre with the support of the members at Bethany Baptist Church.

However, God had still more plans for His servants.

Chapter 21

Honey From the Bee

It is not every mother who has the privilege and awesome responsibility of rearing two families of more than three dozen children. It is even more daunting when that mother has only one son and almost forty daughters. Some mothers might even find it difficult to remember all their names, never mind coping with their needs; however, Lorena Rusovan not only knows them all as if they were her own children, she rescued most of them from a life of misery and despair.

Lorena is happily married to Daniel Rusovan who was also born into a Christian home. His father died when Daniel was only four years old. Early widowhood put a weighty responsibility on his mother to raise her two sons. His father's premature death also helped shape their elder son, Daniel, to be a very responsible and honourable young man. He and Lorena have known each other since they were at kindergarten in their small town on the Serbian/Romanian border. After they married God blessed their home with the arrival of their own son, Paul.

Lorena's daughters are the girls at the Deborah House Centre. She rescued most of them individually, nurtured and supervised their care from their infancy to their Christian adulthood. Of course, she did not do this alone. Around her and under her direction was a fine team of helpers, social workers and counsellors plying their skills and energies to guide and shape the diverse and complicated lives of these girls whom the Lord had placed in their trust.

The Deborah House family is very diverse. Some of the girls were saved from their vulnerable backgrounds as infants while others arrived as young teenagers and were spared the possible fate of prostitution. After supervising, caring, counselling and educating the girls until they graduate from high school, the Deborah House ministry is there to help them get started in adulthood and independence.

One of the big challenges for institutionalised adolescents is the transition from the establishment to independent living. These young girls had little or no experience of buying their weekly groceries, paying monthly utilities or managing a house. Lorena and her friends instruct and assist the girls to find employment, carry responsibility and re-enter society.

In normal situations of state orphanages the insecurity of this transition often leads to violent confrontations and abandonment of hope. Sadly, in too many cases many of these juveniles turn to drug or alcohol dependency, crime or exploitation. With no childhood parental role model to guide them they move out into the world without a basic understanding of normal family life and adult responsibilities.

Recognising these problems for the wider community, the MLI team set up an orientation programme, which they called "Aspirations". This programme was devised by the ministry team at Deborah House and was designed to provide assistance to at-risk youth. The Aspirations course includes psychological analysis, training in social skills and family counselling with some limited financial assistance. Tutoring is also provided for job application and interview skills. University scholarships are made available to those girls who have demonstrated a desire to work and to succeed academically. The principal goal for each Aspirations participant is to become a functioning, independent, and self-supporting young adult who can be fully integrated into Romanian society.

Quite a few girls from the Deborah House Centre were successful in gaining entrance into university, and for this MLI provided them with a monthly allowance through the four or five years of the university course. Other girls opted for training in vocational skills or going directly into employment.

The Deborah House Centre has two apartments in Timisoara which they make available to these girls to help them get started. Thereafter, the friends at Deborah House will pray for, monitor, counsel and help keep them on the right path. No girl is encouraged to be lazy, but if it is perceived that one is becoming somewhat wayward the Deborah House staff is on hand to help that girl.

Nothing gives Lorena and the staff at Deborah House more satisfaction than to see a girl who had been abandoned on the streets of Timisoara or suffered abuse in a home or an institution be nurtured, cared for, trained and loved at Deborah House and turn out to be a lovely Christian young woman. That was Lorena's original aim.

The six-year old girl who Lorena originally discovered when pursuing a boy's birth certificate came all the way through the Deborah House programme. Today she is a fine young Christian lady, a wife and a loving mother whose child went to kindergarten at Bethany Baptist Church. This story can be replicated many times over.

Stanley Barnes was touched one day when one of those young ladies, a product of the Deborah House ministry and married to a fine Christian man, said to him, "Mr. Barnes, when I have a baby I will not abandon it like my mother did to me. I will love him and keep him."

She and her husband now love their baby boy and bring him up in the fear of the Lord in their Christian home.

There is a healthy fraternity amongst the girls who have graduated from the Deborah House Centre. Most of them are keen to support and encourage each other and have great enjoyment in attending each other's weddings and family functions. Most of their weddings take place at Bethany Baptist Church.

Because of her original responsibility at the Onesimus Christian Home for Boys and then founding and directing the work to rescue abused infants and young girls, Lorena's supervising and administrative skills helped widen the ministry of MLI. To sustain and legitimise the ministry at Deborah House, Lorena devoted more time to raising sponsorship for the project inside Romania as well as abroad. Much attention also needed to be given to obtaining legal licences and approval from the local authorities for the custody of each girl admitted to Deborah House. These processes were very time consuming.

Lorena was therefore invited to take on a wider responsibility to coordinate the expanding ministries MLI was developing. One of these agencies over which Lorena was made coordinator was named, "Harmony" which was set up to take the Gospel through music and Bible stories to other at-risk children from government institutions, at schools for special needs children, in juvenile prisons and the remote Romanian villages.

The Harmony project was created in 2005 when Pastor Eugen invited Doru and Rodica Racovicean to accompany a church group to visit the Buzias Juvenile Prison in Timisoara. They were shocked to discover that the prison was bulging with young delinquents who had been involved in criminal activities, ended up on the wrong side of the law and were now placed behind bars.

The MLI's recognised concern and social help for the underprivileged in Timisoara helped the team gain open access to visit these wayward young men in this grim place. Lorena soon began to coordinate visits to the prison with social and spiritual help for the inmates. When visitors arrived from the United States and Great Britain, Eugen introduced them to the young men and gave opportunities to the visitors to sing, testify and preach the Gospel of the Lord Jesus Christ to the imprisoned young men.

The team proved that the amazing grace of God still abounds to the chief of sinners. This was evident in this prison ministry. Even though these juvenile prisoners were incarcerated for the wrongs they had done against society, quite a few genuinely trusted Jesus Christ as Saviour.

Lorena works alongside Doru and Rodica in coordinating Harmony's outreach as they continue to be involved and help in other institutions like that at the Buzias Juvenile Prison. In fact, Harmony's prison Gospel-orientated programme has made such a positive impact in helping lower the repeat offender rates that the prison authorities requested MLI to expand their ministry and make these same programmes available to other young offenders.

MLI's work through Harmony is not limited to prisons. The workers have expanded its ministry to meet the desperate need for food supplements, shoes and clothing for needy children from local villages. They also set up an educational programme to help prevent the children of the poorest families in these villages, especially the ethnic Rroma children from being abandoned or deprived of school. Because of discrimination, truancy laws are not regularly enforced in the rural Rroma villages where authorities choose to ignore the socially unacceptable Rroma people.

Besides giving material aid to these deprived people, MLI workers are seeking to break the centuries-old cycle of disease, hunger, poverty, and child abuse in Rroma villages by giving them an education through their Gospel programmes. They recognise that Christian instruction is the most sustainable investment they can make. An education, once received, can never be negated or retracted.

Another aspect of the Harmony ministry is visiting other orphanages. Sadly, many of these public and private institutions, most drab and bleak, are the only homes many of these children will ever know. During the visits the Harmony team brings the joy of music to the children. No music programme is provided in most of these orphanages due to lack of resources, therefore, Harmony offers to train their choirs. At Christmas and Easter each year, Harmony endeavours to bring all the choirs together from the various orphanages for special programmes.

As she continued to coordinate the various branches of MLI's activities, it broke Lorena's heart that Deborah House could not provide accommodation for all the unfortunate young girls who needed to be rescued from their appalling and hopeless circumstances. This dilemma constrained Lorena and the MLI Board members to consider an extension of the Deborah House ministry. They observed the biblical principle that faith without works is dead, therefore, as soon as they began to ask the Lord to provide a place, they also began to look around for suitable property.

In August 2009, all the girls from the Deborah House with the staff and the staff's families spent two weeks in Northern Ireland at the generous invitation of the friends at Hillsborough. In the evenings the girls visited the churches and sang as an expression of their appreciation for all the generosity that had been shown to them. During the day they visited the beautiful scenic areas of Ulster. The whole group was invigorated by the fantastic care, love and hospitality they had experienced during their visit to the Emerald Isle and returned home to Romania to be ready for their new school year.

The generous help they received from the Free Presbyterian churches in Northern Ireland and the MLI partners in United States was supplemented by funds Lorena raised from friends in Romania. With these donations MLI was able to procure a suitable property in Giarmata, fifteen kilometres northeast of Timisoara, to open another home for girls. This new home, which was known as Deborah House Centre 2, provided a loving sanctuary for another thirty girls who had been spared a life of deprivation and abuse on the streets of Timisoara or in a non-Christian institution.

The Deborah House Centre has ministered to very young girls who had been condemned and victimised by society, but are now loved by caring and devoted Christians who provide them with a home where they can find everything they did not receive from their own families. These dedicated workers at the Deborah House Centre also endeavour to furnish these girls with the skills they will need to help them live an independent and successful life and begin to be the people God intended them to be.

From small beginnings this work has flourished. God had been so good to these dedicated workers and the girls entrusted to their care.

Chapter 22

Harmony Makes Melody

The founders of the "Harmony" project, Doru and Rodica Racovicean, emerged from the long nightmare of communism to bring the Gospel through music and Bible stories not only to government orphanages but also to a school for special needs children and to a juvenile prison. This gifted couple chose to dedicate their considerable talents and to invest their lives by helping boys and girls from disadvantaged backgrounds in Timisoara and the surrounding districts. Their aim was to use their musical talents to bring Gospel harmony to children whose lives were previously blighted by abuse, abandonment, starvation and extreme poverty.

Doru tells his own story:

> I was born into a Christian home in Timisoara. Since my infancy I have been attending church and Sunday school, and as a child I took part in all the children's programmes of the church.
>
> Since my earliest years I have been involved in music. When I was fourteen years old I began to play in the church orchestra, and at seventeen years old I was leading the men's choir. However, I did not become a Christian until I was eighteen years old. For me, conversion was more a process rather than a one off decision. For a long time I stumbled at the simplicity of the Gospel. I always felt I had to do something. I could not see that salvation was by faith alone. It was a happy day when the simple truth of salvation through grace and by faith dawned upon me. I was so grateful to

God that I was trusting in the Lord Jesus Christ as my Saviour.

With newfound vigour I served the Lord in the church and was leading both the men's and the mixed voice choirs.

Two years after I became Christian I became engaged to Rodica who also came from a Christian home. Rodica was born in Braila, which is about 800 kilometres from Timisoara in eastern Romania. We were engaged in March 1983 and were married in June of the same year. Next to salvation, to have Rodica was the greatest gift I have ever received. In time the Lord gave us three more wonderful gifts when He blessed us with three lovely daughters. We did our best to rear them to fear the Lord and to instruct them in the way of salvation through Jesus Christ.

We have been blessed beyond our expectations to see our girls serving the Lord in the church choirs. All that God has given us is because of His mercy and nothing of our merit. From the time the girls were small we taught them to play musical instruments, and through time they also became part of the church orchestra.

In 1990 Rodica and I began to work in an orphanage in Recas, which housed 127 boys, all of whom had varying degrees of mental deficiency. Although working with children was not my passion or ambition, Rodica was different, she always had a big heart for the children in these institutions. One day I was invited to teach Christian songs to the children of this orphanage. My sister was a music teacher, and she told me how difficult it was to teach normal children. I was used to working with an orchestra and an adult choir, but I was dismayed to discover that these children had no appreciation of music, instrumental or vocal.

Given the conditions in which these children were being held did not help them to sing or to value music. Besides the institution being drab and cold, these little ones had no food and only a few threadbare clothes. Furthermore, for most of their lives they had been kept in isolation from society and had no rapport with families in the outside world. They had never been loved. It was no wonder it was hard for these children to sing.

It was then I realised that it was not music these children needed. They needed to hear about the love of God. How that Jesus loves them and died for them on Calvary. When I began to speak to them from the Bible and tell them about the Saviour and how He loves them, they began to respond. It was a miracle for me to see how the Lord began to change these young lives.

Within eighteen months they were not only singing, they had learned more than thirty songs in different languages. The staff at the orphanage could not believe it, and when the director and professors at the school heard them sing they thought it was miraculous. Jesus Christ had made a difference in these children.

It was at that time that we received an invitation from Rev. Stanley Barnes and the friends at Hillsborough Free Presbyterian Church to take the choir to Northern Ireland. I remember the pleasure we had of presenting the children to the Christian congregations in Ulster. People had heard and seen so much on television about Romania's orphans and were obviously expecting to see a group of badly handicapped and downtrodden boys. The shame of Romania had been the horrific images of neglected children. However, this group of boys from the Recas orphanage represented Romania very well.

I remember on one occasion I had to meet a delegation of parliamentary official leaders in Timisoara. One of them was an elder and an experienced man of the government, and after hearing the boys sing, he said to me, "You are the true representatives of Romania when you travel abroad."

Rodica and I continued to work in the orphanage at Recas, and our three girls also came along to help. We tried to be an example to the children so they could see what family life was like. We wanted to impart our family values to them. Those boys did not know how a family functioned or the mutual love relationships that hold a home together. They did not have fathers and mothers, and they had never heard someone say to them, "I love you."

We counted our time there with those boys as an honour to be able to tell them about the Lord Jesus and show them a better way of life. God had placed us in a very special place, and it was a pleasure to be able to influence them and many others with the Gospel of Jesus Christ.

In 1992 Rodica and I were invited to an orphanage for girls in Lugoj.

There were 250 girls in this institution. In our experience, every orphanage situation is challenging, but with 250 girls it is even more challenging. However, over the next two years we were able to find thirty of those girls who had good voices. We worked with them three times each week and taught them many songs as we had done in Recas. We also told them about the Lord Jesus Christ and God's love for them.

After teaching them for two years we received another invitation from Rev. Barnes to visit the churches in Northern Ireland and let the girls sing out the Gospel in their own language and in English. As on our previous visit to Ulster with the boys from Recas, the girls also had a great time and represented their orphanage home very well. They were touched by the outpouring of love from the people who received them.

Some of those girls with whom we worked at that time have gone on to become medical doctors, accountants and professional individuals in other positions. We kept in touch with them during their university years, and they never forgot their visits to Ulster or the great days they had with the choir.

In 1994 we resigned from that orphanage and went to work with MLI in the Onesimus Boys' Home. That was a very specialised ministry, for these boys had been rescued from a destructive lifestyle on the streets of Timisoara. Most of them had never heard about God or the love of the Lord Jesus Christ.

Rodica used to cut their hair to befriend them. I took time to teach the Gospel and tell them of the Saviour. Our three daughters often came to play their musical instruments, and very soon the boys were singing the great truths of the Bible. In 1999 we had the privilege of going to Northern Ireland for the third time and taking these boys with us.

In 2004 we went to work in Buzias Juvenile Penitentiary where we are still working to this day. This is a very special work for us for we have the opportunity to preach the Gospel to the sixty-five young criminals and to the prison officers. Other prisoners who are on release also come back to the prison, and we have opportunity to speak to them too.

When we arrived I carried out a poll among the interns and discovered that 90% of these juvenile delinquents had no church connection whatsoever.

Over the years we have established regular meetings at which we teach them the Word of God. On Sunday mornings we conduct a regular church meeting in the prison, and for this service we are able to invite outside speakers. Our friends from Northern Ireland have also been able to visit the prison to testify and speak to the young people. What I find very interesting is that the prison officers not only attend these services, but they listen to the Word of God and join in the singing.

My goal is to help these boys understand who God is and what His Word teaches concerning the way of salvation. I believe the Bible has the power to change lives. Because of that, I help them learn Bible verses by heart. We endeavour to teach them in a very simple way about the love of God. Some of these lads can memorise the Scriptures very quickly while others are slower. I try to motivate them by offering them a piece of chocolate when they have memorised a verse.

One young man kept admiring my Bible which had a nice soft cover and a concordance. Even though he had a New Testament he made it clear that he would like to have my Bible. I tried to discourage him from asking, but he persisted. I finally gave in and challenged him that if he was able to memorise all of Psalm 119 I would let him have this Bible. I was quite sure the challenge would be too great for him. Two weeks later he returned to tell me he had memorised half of the Psalm. I still held out on the challenge that it had to be all of the 176 verses in the Psalm.

One of the men from Bethany Baptist was with me when this young lad said he had already learned half of the Psalm. This friend added, "If you learn all of the Psalm, he will give you his Bible, and I will give you a bicycle."

Within a month he returned to me one Monday and announced that although he had learned the whole Psalm by heart, he still might need a little help. Not wanting to part with my Bible, I told him that he could only win it if he was able to quote the Psalm without any prompting or outside help.

On Friday he stood up in the class and said, "Professor Doru, you have always been a man of your word so I hope you can keep it this time also. I have learned Psalm 119 and would like to quote it to you."

After class I sat down with my open Bible to listen to this student fluently recite to me the whole Psalm. I followed him verse after verse and by the time he got to 100 verses he had stolen my heart, and with it, he had won my prized possession - my lovely new Bible. He continued to quote the verses and made a mistake only when he skipped a verse near the end of the chapter. I had no alternative but to part with my cherished Bible and the bright young lad also gained a bicycle. Good for him.

I used to tell the young people at Bethany Baptist that we should have a contest between the boys in the church and those in the prison precinct. I had no doubt that the young offenders would know more Bible verses than the young people in the church.

Every day the prisoners have a two-hour recreational break when they are free to engage in all sorts of sports or other interests. It is at that time that I arrange an hour to study the Bible with whoever wants to come; we are amazed how many of these young lads who have come from damaged backgrounds opt to attend the Bible Study hour. This mystifies some psychologists who visit the prison, and they have tried to analyse why the boys would chose to attend a Bible study in preference to a game of tennis or football.

Learning the Scriptures has had a profound effect on many of their lives. News of the change in these young criminals has already reached the government, and they have given us their full approval. I was recently invited to attend a government symposium where there were twenty-five representatives of many other penal institutions. Each one had to give a report of what was happening in their precinct. I was able to tell them of how so many boys had been changed by the influence of the Word of God.

Rodica and I are working full-time with MLI and divide our week between the orphanages, the juvenile prisons and children-at-risk centres. Each Sunday we conduct a Gospel service in one of these institutions.

Since 1990 we have been working with the children for special outreaches at Christmas and Easter. None of these children had ever known what Christmas meant, nor did they have any understanding of Easter and its meaning. While we were working with the large orphanage in Recas in 1990 we asked the friends at Bethany Baptist Church if we could have an Easter celebration for our orphan children. We brought scores of children from different orphanages to sing and quote poetry at a special meeting. The church then treated them to a sumptuous banquet of lamb. Lamb meat is the traditional Easter meal in Romania, and these children were having it for the first time.

At Christmas the church repeated the same exercise with the children blessing the congregation with a great musical programme of carols and songs about the Saviour. This was followed by the children enjoying the church's kind hospitality with plenty of Christmas fare. Over the years these Christmas and Easter celebrations have become very popular annual events for the children and for the church. We have also widened the scope for these celebrations and are now drawing 300 children from Buzias, Lugoj and Recas.

We are grateful to have been able to devote these years to bring the harmony of the Gospel to all these young people. My wife and our daughters have been 100% with me in all that we do.

Doru and Rodica Racovicean continue to be a vital part of the MLI mission outreach through their musical ministry.

--ooO0oo--

John Costache and his wife, Eleana, have also been a vital part of the MLI ministry. Both of them were raised in Christian homes in Bucharest and came to know the Lord Jesus personally in their early lives. During the communist years, like many other Christians in Romania, they had to trust in God under the most stressful situations. However, God helped them, and they emerged from those oppressive years much stronger in their faith. Their son is called Andrew.

When John was five years old some Christians in his church encouraged him to enter a singing contest that had been organised by Romanian State television. They were really auditioning for one of the best children's choirs in the whole country. The choir, composed of 250 children, had been in existence for about ten years at that time, so they needed a new generation of voices. About 300 girls and 150 boys entered for the competition. Only fifty-seven of these were eventually selected for the choir.

John was one of twelve boys accepted by the directors of the choir. To be a member of this choir was considered to be very prestigious, and he really did feel honoured. They had two rehearsals every week and were paid a reasonable monthly allowance.

At Christmas and Easter and on national days the choir was required to sing all sorts of songs for the upper echelons of Romanian society and ministers of the government, including President Ceausescu. During his nine years with the choir John sang in Ceausescu's palace on five or six occasions.

John's voice broke when he was fourteen years old, and he had to leave the choir. He was soon selected for another prestigious and famous Romanian national choir, but John had accepted the Lord Jesus Christ as his Saviour when he was seventeen years old, and his life had been changed.

Singing with the choir and professing Jesus Christ would soon bring a conflict of interests for John. During his time with this well-acclaimed choir, pressure was put on him to become a member of the Communist Party. They guaranteed that, as a member of the party, new doors would open to him in the music world. He resisted this pressure and courageously told them that he was a Christian, and therefore, he could not be a member of the party or be a communist. However, he offered to continue to sing with the choir if they were prepared to respect his Christian faith and values, but if not, he would accept their decision. Soon afterwards he was dismissed from that choir.

John's mother had always been a great encourager and counsellor to him and especially at that time. She taught him that it was much more important to sing for the glory of God than for the praise of man. From then on John dedicated his life to sing the Gospel of the Lord Jesus Christ.

In the mid-seventies John and Eleanor met Pastor Petru Dugulescu in Bucharest, and he invited them to Timisoara to help in the Gospel ministry. Following the Romanian Revolution they became part of the Onesimus Christian Boys' Home to help rescue young men from destroying their lives through crime and drugs on the streets of Timisoara.

In 2001 John and Eleanor joined with Pastor Eugen Groza and the MLI team in the children-at-need outreach out of which Deborah House was founded. It was obvious that through the Onesimus programme the Lord had been preparing the couple for this ministry among abused girls. Although they were ready for anything that was required of them, John's role was very much taken up with the administrative side of the work. He takes care of all the legal and financial interests of the ministry.

The great passion of John's life is to sing and to help others sing also. He has a rich tenor voice which he uses in the service of the Lord all over the world. He works alongside Doru and Rodica Racovicean in the Harmony ministry by helping prepare the girls' choir. He always plays a big part in their various celebrations, and nothing gives him greater pleasure than to help these girls discover their musical and vocal gifts.

John became a very popular and well-loved Gospel singer with the Free Presbyterian Churches during the visits the various choirs made to Ulster. The Christian public in Northern Ireland, who know John by the more endearing "Little John", have greatly acclaimed the CD audio recordings of his best-loved hymns. Amongst these favourites are: The Holy City, How Great Thou Art, His Eye is on the Sparrow and Because He Lives. John confesses that the greatest experience of his life is to see hearts being touched while he sings about the love of God and having the joy of some people coming to faith in Christ through this ministry.

--ooOOoo--

Romania, like most of Eastern Europe, remains a country in transition. The MLI ministries today have adapted their outreach to extend throughout Romania and reach into the neighbouring countries of Moldova, Ukraine and Serbia. Their missionary work continues among abused children, orphans, juvenile offenders, children at risk and with the elderly in Timisoara, Lugoj, Recas and Giarmata. They have opened a multipurpose conference and retreat centre in the Transylvanian Alps for youth evangelism, discipleship and leadership development. Under Eugen's presidency MLI coordinates an intensive training programme for more than 340 Christian leaders in strategic areas in south and northeast Romania.

Thousands of Romanians paid a heavy price for the freedoms they now enjoy, some paid with the ultimate sacrifice of their lives. For decades Christians had to endure martyrdom, torture, imprisonment, persecution and constant harassment. All of that has changed. For more than ten years they have been entrusted with freedom. Eugen and his friends are conscious that this liberty brings with it great opportunity and an awesome responsibility. They want to make the best use of the opportunities God has given to them.

Eugen once remarked, "To live for Christ is sometimes more difficult than to be willing to die for Christ."

Pray for Pastor Eugen. He and his wife Mihaela continue in their extensive and intensive ministry all over Romania. In 1990, immediately after the revolution, God blessed their home with the arrival of second daughter, Sorina. Later, their first daughter, Adelina, studied computer engineering at the University of Timisoara. She married Jonathan and the Lord blessed their home with two beautiful daughters: Heidi and Hannah. At present Sorina is studying dentistry and plans to marry Daniel in May 2014.

Chapter 23

Treasures of Hope

Horrific stories flow into our homes through the news media of hundreds of children who have been caught up in conflicts and wars all over our world. Sometimes we have been moved to tears on seeing body bags containing small babies and young children who have been killed by indiscriminate bombing or attacks of poison gas. Our hearts have been deeply moved at the sight of scores of despairing children who have been physically maimed or blinded through senseless and savage terrorist attacks on their defenceless communities or by land mines left in the wake of a former war.

When I see these horrendous images or those of emaciated babies in famine stricken regions of Africa, I always think that each one of these little waifs is precious to some mother and father, to some brother and sister. Most of all, the Bible assures us that they are precious to our loving Father in heaven whose eye is even on the little sparrows.

Perhaps, less noticeable, but equally as cruel and destructive, is the damage and harm inflicted on countless scores of children and young people by the diabolical arsenal of Satan. His design has always been the destruction of individuals and the younger they are the better for his strategy. Day after day it comes to light that there are too many boys and girls suffering because they have been neglected and unloved by their families, abandoned or abused by relations, maimed or mangled by society and therefore, left in the depths of hopeless despair. Who can understand their hurt and heartache? Who can give them hope when it seems they are on a dark and downward spiral of misery and gloom?

Lorena Rusovan and the team at Deborah House have dedicated their lives to offer fresh hope and a loving home for the derelict, abused and abandoned children of Timisoara and Western Romania. Besides pouring out compassion upon these young people they also engage in moulding and influencing their lives by a good education, career counselling and teaching them the Word of God. This work does not produce overnight results and is sometimes met with disappointment or frustration. However, there is great satisfaction in seeing many of these young people emerge into adulthood as fine Christian people. When measured against the backgrounds from which they came they truly are the treasures of hope.

Florica was the first girl admitted to Deborah House Centre. She tells her own story;

> I was born into a poor family of seventeen children. I cannot remember any holiday we ever spent together and I cannot recall any pleasant memories of my early childhood. When I was eight years old, I lost my mother. After that, the situation in our family got worse and worse for me until I decided to run away from home. Even though I was only a young girl I worked as a servant for a family and did not go to school. When I was seventeen years old I went to work for another family in Giarmata.

> At that time I heard about the construction of Deborah House Centre and the safety it would provide for young girls like me. I only wished that I could live there, but did not see the possibility. However, this dream did come true and in time I was accepted to live in the Deborah House. Once I was there I had the courage to dream bigger and bigger dreams. Because of the support I received at the Deborah House Centre I was able to finish middle school and then find a job.

> Best of all, in 2004 I received the Lord as my Saviour and I was baptised at Bethany Baptist Church. In 2006, I got married and in 2009 I gave birth to

our little baby girl. She had some medical problems, but with the help of the Missio Link International Foundation, I managed to overcome those hard moments in my life.

At present I am studying in the high school and by God's grace I will graduate in 2015. God has been so good to me. Today I have a beautiful and healthy daughter and a husband who loves me. We both love the Lord and we want our daughter to have the type of parents that we never knew.

There is also the case of a beautiful nineteen year-old girl called Mirela. She relates her personal story;

When I arrived at Deborah House on a very cold winter afternoon, my only possessions were the clothes I was wearing. I came from an extremely poor background. Even as a child I thought that the best thing for me was to study hard at school so that I could escape from my poverty and have a better life. I worked hard at my studies and got a high grade so that I was accepted into the high school in my hometown.

At high school I also tried hard to do my best, but at home I lived in terror. My fears were not because of our poverty, but because my mother was sick and was also alcoholic. She was often absent from home while being treated for her addiction. My father was not much better for he constantly smoked and was more often drunk than sober. With my mother away or being drunk when she was at home, I had to cook for my younger sister, clean the house as best I could and also tend to the animals before and after school. On top of this, because of my father's addiction to alcohol he did not have a regular job so I had to work for a neighbour to provide a little money for the family.

Even though I had all these responsibilities at home I was still able to keep up with my school work. The principal at my high school and my handball coach said that I was the only student who never missed an hour of practice and never skipped a lesson at school.

Since my father was the only one who worked, but only occasionally, I took a job with a neighbour. I was only fourteen years old. The neighbour for whom I worked later became my father's boss and sadly, with my father's consent, he began to abuse me.

I tried to resist him, but when I did this one of the men who was abusing me gave me a very severe beating. I told my mother what was happening so she called the police. Subsequently, my case was placed into the hands of the Child's Welfare Organisation in Timisoara.

This welfare authority introduced my sister and me to the Deborah House Centre. Although we were frightened we were also confident that we would find peace. Very soon I was able to transfer to another good high school in Timisoara from which I graduated in 2013. After graduation I applied to the Faculty of Medicine to become a medical doctor. I am glad to say I was accepted and now I am studying at the University of Arad, a city forty-five kilometres away from Timisoara. Going to university was a big change for me, but at weekends I do not have classes so I travel to Deborah House to spend time with my sister who is still there. Each time I return I feel like I am coming home.

Three years ago I received the Lord Jesus into my heart and asked Him to restore me. Being part of the church in Arad and Timisoara really helps me. In Arad I go to the youth meetings in the church there and when I go to Timisoara for the weekend I attend Bethany Baptist Church because this is my home church. God has been good to me and I know He will not abandon me. I pray that my sister will be saved and allow Him to restore her the way He restored me.

It gives Lorena and her friends great satisfaction to see what the Lord does for these young girls who have been loved and nurtured at the Deborah House Centre. Adnana is another girl who was anxious to tell her story;

I am eighteen years old. After spending more than three years in the care of the Deborah House Centre I was admitted into the Aspirations Program. My biggest desire is to accomplish something professionally and to become an independent person. I love to work with children and while I was still living at the Deborah House I obtained a baby-sitting and child-care qualification. Shortly afterwards I moved into one of the Aspirations flats in Timisoara.

Now as an independent person I have several part-time jobs baby-sitting and cleaning houses. I also attend high school evening classes. I am determined to pass the Baccalaureate exam and be able to find a good job. One of the biggest regrets in my life is that on three occasions I refused to go to the Deborah House Centre. If I had done so initially I would have graduated from high school by now. I have three little sisters and they have a very hard life. I would love for them also to enter the Deborah House Centre until I am able to find a permanent job. After that I will take care of them. My greatest wish is to rescue my three younger sisters from the place from which I ran away.

Simona, a twenty-two year-old student of International Relations, wrote after about her gratitude to Deborah House and the Aspirations Project;

I cannot say I had a happy childhood. Both of my parents died when I was very young. I was passed through many courts for the authorities to establish my legal custody, I was taken from the Lugoj Children's Home and entrusted to my sister. From there I was sent to another family before I finally arrived at the Deborah House Centre. During all this time I never knew what it was to belong to a family. I went to elementary school and then the high school where I successfully passed the exams. In 2012 I graduated from the University of Timisoara with a degree in Economics and International Affairs

Back in 2004 I accepted the Lord Jesus Christ as Saviour and afterwards I was baptised at Bethany Baptist Church. While at a youth meeting at the Bethany Church I met the person who became my husband. How good the Lord is for I now have a job and a large family. My husband has nine siblings so when we were married all of them became my brothers and sisters. My dreams to have a family of my own became a reality. However, I must confess that I miss the family I had while I was at Deborah House. It was the place where I really felt I was loved unconditionally.

I am glad I had the chance to start an independent life with the help and support of all those involved in this work. All of my results obtained in college are because of you. Thank you for all your support and, especially, for your love.

Elena is a twenty-one year-old young lady. When she was ten years old she was entrusted to a foster family. This was because of the neglect she and her sister suffered at the hands of their alcoholic mother. The poor lady had no income and she slept with her two girls in a deserted train wagon.

The foster family provided a home for Elena for seven years but those were seven years of unmentionable abuse to the young girl. It was then that the welfare authority stepped in and eventually transferred Elena to the custody and care of the staff at Deborah House. For her, a new life had begun. As with all the young residents entrusted to their care, seventeen-year-old Elena was introduced to a good high school. The trauma of her troubled past had left deep psychological scars on Elena's mental state and although she was academically bright, she struggled with several psychotic episodes.

At Deborah House Elena underwent three years of counselling, psychotherapy and medication. She graduated from high school with very good distinction and successfully passed her baccalaureate.

With the aid of the Aspirations Project Elena was able to leave Deborah House and develop her independent living and social skills with limited financial support from the Deborah House Foundation. She moved into a secure apartment and gained a job in commerce. Elena's future plans are to follow a nursing career.

Another young twenty year-old who has emerged from the Deborah House and Aspirations Project is Claudia, a cosmetician, who wrote, "My life was not easy. I did not have a happy childhood. Thanks to Deborah House, I can go to school and have a future life, so, thanks for everything you gave me."

Gabriela who is now a hairdresser also adds her appreciation for the care and compassion poured into her life, "Because of you I have prepared to start my independent life. I was able to live in a single household, learn to manage my money and cope with many other situations of daily life. Above all, I have been supported and helped to find the family

I dreamed of. Thank you for caring for me for I have been taught and guided so well."

These are only a few of the testimonies of those girls who have been blessed and advanced through the 'Children at Risk' Programme of the Missio Link International. Mike and Darlene McKeithen volunteered to help in the work at Deborah House and Mike is the Chairman of the Mission International Board in USA. They wrote the following about their involvement:

> We have been familiar with the work of Deborah House since it first opened in the summer of 2002. During those first few years when we went with mission teams to help at Deborah House we were very impressed by the programme and the professionalism of Lorena and her staff.

> Seven years ago we became active volunteers. We did this primarily because of the outstanding results of the Deborah House programme for we could see a positive change in the Deborah girls. Secondly, we also wanted to be supportive of Lorena and her staff and their successful programme. It has made a real and demonstrative difference in the lives of the Deborah House girls.

> We have also had first hand experience of the positive results in the lives of those who have benefited from the Aspirations Project, the Harmony and the Back to School programmes of the Missio Link's Children at Risk ministries.

> It has been a privilege and a very real blessing to have played a small role with others in supporting Lorena and her staff in these and other successful programmes.

Pastor Eugen, Lorena and all the other workers on the ground have been greatly encouraged to have had the support of friends from around the world in helping them rescue these precious young lives from the dark alleyways of cruel abuse and empty hopelessness to provide them with a home, with compassion and a hopeful future.

Chapter 24

Holding the Ropes

Working with children, your own or others, can be unpredictable, amusing, hilarious and often annoyingly frustrating. However, these precious little people can occasionally come out with some rare pearls of wisdom. That is exactly what happened when one little boy hung around to help his father with a chore at home. After the job was completed the young son, feeling he had played an important part, looked up at his dad and remarked, "Daddy, when I try to do things by myself they always seem to go wrong. But when you and I work together they turn out just right."

Christian fellowship and generous partnership have characterised this remarkable work in Romania since before the Revolution of December 1989. The commitment and kindness of bighearted and openhanded friends at Hillsborough and elsewhere in Northern Ireland have enhanced the close bonds that have led to the expansion of God's work and the furtherance of the Gospel in that country.

The Scriptures remind us that Christians are not only expected to be workers, but to be workers together with God. In the New Testament believers are not likened to only a building, they are also likened to a body - each one baptised into the body of Christ. Every member of that body needs and depends on all the other members functioning under its common Head, who is Jesus Christ.

This principle was amply illustrated in the life and ministry of the apostle Paul. Immediately after his conversion he entered into Damascus. It was there he began to speak and testify that Jesus was the Christ. The fact that this feared persecutor who had set out to exterminate all those who were disciples of Christ in Damascus, was now publicly proclaiming Christ caused immense consternation among the Jews. Their rage was so extreme that they decided to eliminate him by putting him to death.

Did Paul feel vulnerable when his life was in danger? Did he feel exposed to peril since he had forsaken those with whom he had so ardently identified in their opposition and persecution of Christians? Could he find refuge amongst those who just a few days earlier had been his target for extermination? Could he trust them?

Under God's providential direction, it was the corporate commitment, loving fellowship and practical partnership of those Syrian Christians in the city that rescued the apostle from his menacing predators: *"And after that many days were fulfilled, the Jews took counsel to kill him: But their laying await was known of Saul. And they watched the gates day and night to kill him. Then the disciples took him by night, and let him down by the wall in a basket"* (Acts 9:23-25).

We do not know the names of those disciples in Damascus or how many of them risked their lives and reputations to come to the aid of the apostle. We do know that they played a vital role in the preservation of Paul's life. They were prepared to extend their Christian compassion to this one-time enemy and persecutor. Their commitment was such that they were prepared to meet in the middle of the night and courageously put their own lives at risk for the sake of this new convert. We do not read of the gifts and abilities of these men, if indeed they were all men. We do know that they were committed enough to play a practical role by holding the ropes for the man of God who was prepared to get into the basket.

Paul also must have looked into the faces of these new friends and brothers in Christ as he climbed into the basket. He needed to have the confidence that they would not only hold on to the ropes, but that they would not slacken their grip until the basket touched the ground. That is exactly what they did.

That night in Damascus those followers of Jesus Christ displayed the excellent qualities expressed by one sage who said, "The Christian's best ability is his dependability." Paul was able to count on those anonymous, but dependable disciples. His life and future depended on their vital and sacrificial contribution.

Those early disciples could not have known the potential of the man of God who was in their basket. The man they supported that night became the greatest Christian who has ever lived, the greatest missionary the church has ever known and the human author of almost half of our New Testament.

Throughout Paul's life and ministry he worked in unison with a vast company of co-workers. In Romans chapter 16 he greets twenty-six different companions who contributed support and encouragement to the life of the apostle. He needed them.

All the self-effacing qualities displayed by Paul's anonymous friends on that perilous night in Damascus have been replicated in the wide network of supporters and participants who have been holding the ropes for the varied ministries of MLI under the leadership of Pastor Eugen Groza. These modern day rope-holders have played a significant role in enhancing the work of the Gospel and encouraging God's servants as they help and serve the needy people of Romania.

The friendship formed between Pastor Eugen Groza and Rev. Stanley Barnes was the precursor to the links and bonds that would be established between their respective churches, Bethany Baptist Church in Timisoara and Hillsborough Free Presbyterian Church in Northern Ireland. Though separated by many miles, both churches and their members have enjoyed a warm relationship and have mutually benefited and been blessed by the frequent exchange visits to Romania and Northern Ireland.

While Stanley was minister at the Hillsborough Church, he and his wife, Ina, organised the repeated trips to Ulster for the underprivileged boys and girls and their carers from the Recas and Lugoj orphanages and the Onesimus and Deborah Christian Homes. Stanley and Ina readily confess that they could not have undertaken to arrange these visits, if it had not been for the love, unstinting support and hard work of the members of his congregation. They were always willing and ready to rise to the occasion of entertaining, transporting and sharing with the children.

Since Stanley's retirement from Hillsborough, the Rev. Gary Goods, the present minister of the church, the office bearers and congregation continue to give their full unstinting support in hosting the visiting Romanian groups to Ulster.

A final word expresses Stanley's gratitude for all these ministries and their supporters:

> Looking back over the past twenty-four years we rejoice in what the Lord has accomplished. Truly with the Psalmist we can say, "This is the Lord's doing; it is marvellous in our eyes" (Psalm 118: 23). In publishing this account we trust that the reader will be stirred to praise God with us for His goodness. Almighty God chooses to use men and women as His instruments to fulfil His purposes. The pages of this book therefore, contain the story of what has been accomplished through faithful believers who have held the ropes for this ministry in so many ways.

> The well-known and loved passage in Hebrews 11 has often been termed the "Hall of Fame" or the "Roll of Honour" of men and women of faith. Not so well known is the "Roll of Honour" of equally diligent workers contained in Nehemiah chapter 3. God knows every one of His servants, and of each we conclude with the writer to the Hebrews, "...of whom the world was not worthy."

It would be impossible to mention all the names of those who have contributed to the work and witness of Deborah House in Romania. However, it is good to remember that "God is not unrighteous to forget your work and labour of love, which ye have shewed toward His name..." (Hebrews 6:10). No one will be omitted from that "Book of Remembrance" being written in heaven - (Malachi 3:16).

Beside each name will be recorded the individual deeds of kindness and the Lord's acknowledgement in Matthew 25:40 that, "Inasmuch as ye have done it unto one of the least of these my brethren, ye have done it unto me."

It is amazing to think how Stanley's visit to Romania came about. Immediately after the Romanian Revolution in December 1989, Tom Lewis invited his friend Pastor Doru Popa from Arad, Romania, to visit churches in Northern Ireland. During his two weeks in Ulster in January 1990, Pastor Doru's presentation and preaching made a mighty impact wherever he went. All who heard him responded very positively, and before returning home, the pastor asked Tom to invite Dr. Paisley, William McCrea and Victor Maxwell to visit him and his church in Romania.

Stanley had always been interested in the work of Romania, and one Friday at the lunch hour open-air meeting in front of Belfast's City Hall, he asked Dr. Paisley if there was any possibility of being included in the delegation. To this Dr. Paisley replied with a smile, "Yes, come and buy your own ticket."

That ticket was money well spent. That compassion was love well spent.

Truly we can say with John Newton, "God moves in mysterious ways."